HEAL YOUR MIND HEAL YOUR LIFE

CORINNE COE

"Butterflies are a symbol of resurrection, hope, joy, and new beginnings. It is a symbol of rebirth and a transformation of change. Just like a caterpillar must go through several growth and development before it can become a beautiful butterfly, so must we go through several growth experiences in life before we experience our true purpose and get to a place of inner peace in life."

Dr Amy Hymes

COPYRIGHT & MEDICAL DISCLAIMER

This book is a work of non-fiction based on life, experience and recollections of the author and in some cases those who have gone before. In some cases, names of people have been changed to protect the privacy of others. The author states that, except in such respects, the contents of this manual are accurate and true according to her memory of events.

The author of this book does not dispense medical advice or prescribe the use of any technique as a form of treatment for physical, emotional, or medical problems without the advice of a physician, either directly or indirectly. The 'intent' of the author is only to offer information of a general educative nature to help you in your quest for emotional and psychological well-being. In the event you use any of the information in this book for yourself, which is your constitutional right, the author and publisher assume no responsibility for your actions.

First published in Australia in its current form in 2016 by Corinne Coe.

Publisher's Website address: www.corinnecoe.com.au

Cover design and typesetting by Green Hill Publishing

ISBN: 978-0-9946431-7-9

FIRST EDITION, 2016

This book is dedicated to anyone who
has struggled with mental illness.

To order another copy of:

HEAL YOUR MIND
HEAL YOUR LIFE

visit

www.corinnecoe.com.au

CONTENTS

PART ONE

THEORY

CHAPTER ONE

OVERVIEW OF MENTAL ILLNESS

A mental illness or disorder is a diagnosable illness that significantly interferes with an individual's cognitive, emotional and/or social abilities. Mental illness is the leading cause of 'healthy life' lost due to disability. The alarming statistics have fueled the increased attention among researchers today to find the answer to the critical question, 'Why are some people more susceptible to developing a mental illness than others?'

> ***About 20% of Adult Australians, or one in five people, will experience a mental illness at some stage in their lives. Many will live with more than one mental illness at a time, such as anxiety and depression, which commonly occur together.***

ACCORDING, to the Australian Bureau of Statistics National Survey of Mental Health and Well-being:

Each year a further 20 000 Australians are found to have a mental illness. In summary:

- Three million Australians will experience a major depressive illness during their lifetime;
- Almost 1 in 100 Australians will experience schizophrenia during their lifetime;
- About 3 per cent of Australians will experience a psychotic illness such as schizophrenia during their lifetime.
- Many of those who experience mental health problems will experience more than one mental illness at the one time, such as depression and anxiety, which commonly occur together.
- Three million Australians will experience a major depressive illness during their lifetime.
- Anxiety disorders are most common, and affected 1 in 7 adults. 5% of Australians experience anxiety so crippling that it affects every aspect of their lives.
- Mental illness has the third highest burden of disease in Australia, followed closely by cancer and cardiovascular disease.
- The overall rate of mental disorders in Australia and Canada is a little lower than that in the US. However, the pattern of mental disorders is consistent with Canada, the US and the UK, with anxiety disorders the most common disorders, followed by substance use disorders and depression.

Young people and mental illness

- The greatest number of people with a mental illness is within the 18-24 year age group.
- Depression is one of the most common health conditions in young people and increases during adolescence.

Gender and mental illness

- Men and women experience similar rates of mental illness.
- Women are more likely than men to experience depression and anxiety disorders, while men are more likely to experience substance abuse.

Depression, one of the most commonly diagnosed psychiatric disorders is being diagnosed in increasing numbers in various segments of the population worldwide, and is often a precipitating factor in suicide. Within the next twenty years depression is expected to become the second leading cause of disability worldwide and the leading cause in high-income nations.

MAJOR DEPRESSION

Depression is a mood state that is characterised by significantly lowered mood and a loss of interest or pleasure in activities that are normally enjoyable. Different types of depression often have slightly different symptoms. The five main types of depression are listed below.

- **Major depression -** a depressed mood that lasts for at least two weeks. This may also be referred to as Clinical Depression or Unipolar Depression.
- **Psychotic depression -** a depressed mood which includes symptoms of psychosis. Psychosis involves seeing or hearing things that are not there (hallucinations), feeling everyone is against you (paranoia) and having delusions.
- **Dysthymia -** a less severe depressed mood that lasts for years.
- **Mixed depression and anxiety -** a combination of symptoms of depression and anxiety.
- **Bipolar disorder -** (formerly known as Manic Depressive Illness) - involves periods of feeling low (depressed) and high (manic).

While it is common and normal to experience 'ups and downs', Depression can be distinguished by its severity, persistence, duration, and the presence of characteristic symptoms. According to the Diagnostic and Statistical Manual of Mental Disorders (DSM-V), for a diagnosis of Depressive Episode the following criteria must be met:

- The Depressive episode is not due to psychoactive substance abuse or any organic mental disorder and,

Two weeks or more of:

- Abnormal lowering of mood *(felt down, depressed, or hopeless)*
- Loss of interest or pleasure in doing things
- Loss of energy

If positive, check for the remaining symptoms:

- Loss of confidence or self-esteem
- Unreasonable feelings of self-reproach or excessive or inappropriate guilt
- Recurrent thoughts of death or suicide, or any suicidal behaviour
- Complaints or evidence of diminished ability to think or concentrate, such as indecisiveness
- Change in psychomotor activity, with agitation or retardation (subjective or objective)
- Sleep disturbance of any type
- Change in appetite with corresponding weight change

Your Score:

If you scored 5 or more, you may have Depression. It is important to note that this checklist provides only a rough guide as to whether someone has a disorder. For a full diagnosis, it is important to **see a doctor.**

The severity of Depression can be classified as ***mild*** *(4 – 5 symptoms)*, ***moderate*** *(6-7 symptoms)*, or ***severe*** *(8-10 symptoms)*, depending on the symptoms' present level of functional impairment.

SEVERITY OF DEPRESSION

In mild depression you will have some symptoms of depression but, with effort, still able to continue with most everyday activities. With mild depression you will experience only minor impairment in occupational and/or social functioning.

Moderate depression involves significant occupational and/or social impairment. You will have many of the symptoms of depression, and have significant difficulty in completing everyday activities.

Severe depression involves marked impairment in these areas and may, but not always include psychotic symptoms. You will have nearly all the symptoms of depression and the depression almost always prevents you from doing your regular day to day activities.

Major depressive episodes can be single, recurrent or chronic. While most sufferers of Depression will experience a remission of their symptoms without treatment, 5 – 10% never recover and experience chronic symptoms. With appropriate treatment, the majority of people will achieve a complete recovery from the current episode.

PROCESS OF THE DEVELOPMENT OF DEPRESSION AND RECOVERY FROM DEPRESSION

The development of Depression commences in what is known as the 'mild' stage and slowly develops into the 'moderate', then 'severe' and in some cases 'extremely severe' stage. The duration of each stage is highly dependent on the individual, the type of treatment and support, and what is going on in their life at the time. As Depression transitions into each stage, so does the intensity of the symptoms of Depression, with the worst effect mostly experienced in the moderate to severe stage.

The process of recovering from Depression occurs in a similar way. For instance, if it starts in the severe stage, over time it should fall into the moderate stage, then mild stage, then into the 'remission' stage, and fi nally fall into the 'recovery' stage. During the recovery process, should an individual relapse, this is highly likely to occur between the Remission and Recovery stage, and spiral back down through each stage. A common cause of relapse, is ceasing treatment prematurely - before the 'Recovery' stage is reached. The diagram on the following page outlines the stages in the development of severe depression, and the stages of recovering from depression, and the common relapse stages.

Increasingly, Depression is recognised as a chronic and recurrent condition. Up to 75% of people diagnosed with Depression will suffer further episodes throughout their life. For example, a mood disorder can be the primary condition to a secondary anxiety disorder and vis versa. Should this be the case, it is important to treat the primary condition as a priority as the secondary condition should resolve itself once the primary condition is treated.

DIAGRAM 1.1

Process of Depression and Recovery

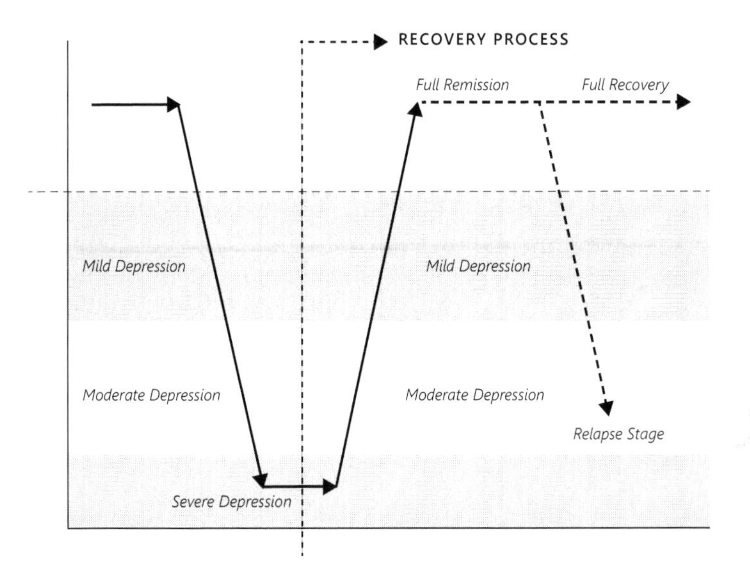

ROLE OF MEDICATION IN MANAGING DEPRESSION

Medication has its place in managing depression particularly, in severe depression and considered to be the first step in treatment. While severe depression can be successfully treated with a combination of medication and therapy, mild to moderate levels of Depression can in a lot of cases be effectively treated with psychological therapy such as Cognitive Behavioural Therapy (CBT) as a first line of treatment before considering medication as part of the treatment. The decision on the most effective treatment options should be made in consultation with a doctor after careful assessment and consideration, as each case is different. A person can help the Doctor make an accurate assessment by being open and providing as much information as possible about themselves and their medical history.

Currently there are about 20 different antidepressant medications on the market. Most antidepressants fall into one of three categories: selective serotonin reuptake inhibitors (SSRIs), tricyclics, or monoamine oxidase inhibitors (MAOIs). First line medications include those in the SSRI family (Selective Serotonin Reuptake Inhibitor) such as, Prozac or Paxil. Prozac, Paxil, and Wellbutrin are the most commonly prescribed SSRIs, and typically have few side effects.

TYPES OF ANTIDEPRESSANTS

There are many different classes of antidepressant medication.

Selective Serotonin Reuptake Inhibitors (SSRIs)

This class includes:

- Sertraline (Zoloft)
- Citalopram (Cipramil, Ciazil, Talohexal)
- Paroxetine (Aropax, Paxtine)
- Fluoxetine (Prozac, Erocap, Lovan, Zactin, Auscap)
- Fluvoxamine (Luvox, Faverin).

SSRIs are:

- The antidepressants most commonly prescribed in Australia
- The most popular first choice for most types of depression among Doctors.
- Effective with fairly few side-effects.

Serotonin and NorAdrenalin Reuptake Inhibitors (SNRIs)

This class includes:

- Venlafaxine (Efexor, Efexor-XR).

SNRIs:

- Have fewer side-effects compared to the older antidepressants.
- Are effective in severe depression.

Reversible inhibitors of monoamine oxidase – (RIMAs)

This class includes:

- Moclobemide (Aurorix, Arima).*RIMAs:*
- Have fairly few side-effects at standard doses but may require higher doses to be fully effective.
- Are non-sedating.
- May be less effective in managing severe depression than some other antidepressants.
- Are helpful in the treatment of anxiety or difficulty sleeping.

Tricyclic antidepressants (TCAs)

This class includes:

- Nortriptyline (Allegron)

- Clomipramine (Anafranil)
- Dothiepin (Prothiaden, Dothep)
- Imipramine (Tofranil)
- Amitriptyline (Tryptanol, Endep).

TCAs are:

- Effective, but have more side-effects than newer drugs
- More likely to cause low blood pressure – so this should be monitored by a doctor.

NorAdrenalin-serotonin specific antidepressants (NaSSAs)

This class includes:

- Mirtazapine (Avanza, Remeron).

NaSSAs are:

- Relatively new antidepressants
- Particularly helpful when there are problems with anxiety or difficulty sleeping
- Generally low in sexual side-effects.

NorAdrenalin reuptake inhibitors (NARIs)

This class includes:

- Reboxetine (Edronax).

NARIs are:

- Designed to act selectively on one type of brain chemical – norAdrenalin – which is associated with improving mood and increasing energy
- Less likely to cause sleepiness or drowsiness than some other Antidepressants
- More likely to make it difficult for people to sleep
- More likely to cause increased sweating after the initial doses, as well as sexual difficulties, difficulty urinating and increased heart rate.

In general, antidepressants work by affecting the transmission of electrical impulses between the brain cells, and each family of antidepressants have a different way of affecting the chemical messengers – known as Neurotransmitters. Different medications may affect different brain chemicals that play an important role in depression. For example, lower levels of the neurotransmitter, 'Serotonin' have been shown to be present when people are depressed.

Although there are other categories of antidepressants, SSRI's are the most commonly prescribed medications for depression. SSRI's act by increasing the amount of serotonin that remains available in the synaptic cleft, so that more of it can be sent successfully between one cell and another. When someone is depressed, there are less brain chemicals available and also less receptor sites in the nerve cells which make it more difficult for the messages to be passed on through. For most people experiencing depression, these subtle but important chemical changes result in a host of physical symptoms.

SSRI's act by blocking the uptake pump that recycles the chemicals (serotonin, dopamine, and noradrenalin) allowing these chemicals to remain around the receptors long enough to be absorbed. The more fish in the lake the greater the chance of catching one.

See Diagram 1.2 below (http://commonantidepressants.weebly.com/selective-serotonin-reuptake-inhibitors.htmlon).

DIAGRAM 1.2

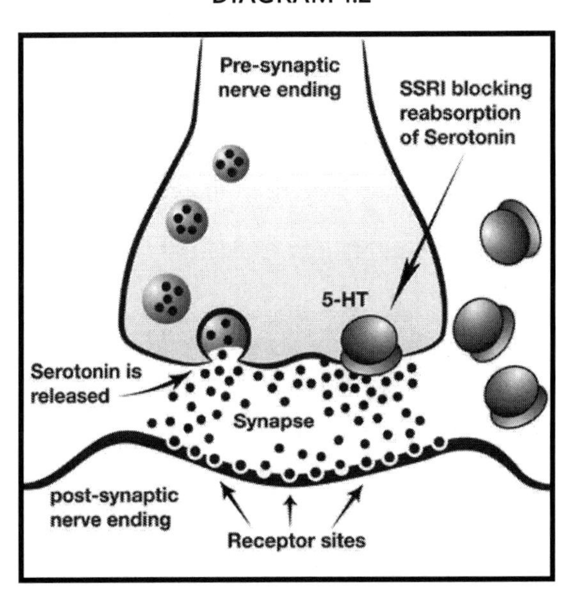

SIDE EFFECTS OF ANTIDEPRESSANTS

Unfortunately, it is not possible to accurately predict which medication may work best for any given individual, and which of the possible side effects may occur. Some people are much more sensitive to medication than others and weighing up tolerating side effects in order to ease the symptoms is something that will need to be taken into consideration when deciding on whether or not to include medication as part of the treatment plan. Research shows that SSRIs are generally safer and have fewer side effects than other antidepressants such as, SNRI (Selective NorAdrenalin Reuptake Inhibitor) e.g., Effexor.

Some of the common side effects of SSRIs include:

- Nausea/Diarrhea
- Difficulty sleeping
- Anxiety
- Sexual dysfunction
- Dry mouth
- Sweating
- Weight Gain

ANXIETY

An Anxiety Disorder is not a matter of 'being too anxious'. The experience of anxiety is necessary and very normal – appropriate levels of anxiety will increase alertness and performance when needed such as, during a job interview, exam or sports performance. Even a higher level of anxiety is necessary to increase arousal and reflexes when faced with a situation where real danger is present. However, when persistent and severe anxiety is experienced without justification, it can be debilitating in that it can affect your ability to process new information, plan and problem-solve, and perform complex activities. When you suffer from an anxiety disorder, you have specific and recurring fears that you recognise as being irrational or unrealistic and intrusive.

There are different types of anxiety disorders including; Panic Disorder, Agoraphobia, Social Phobia, Specific Phobia, Generalised Anxiety Disorder, Obsessive Compulsive Disorder, Adjustment Disorder, Post-Traumatic Stress Disorder, and Acute Stress Disorder.

GAD and Panic Disorder are the most common of all the Anxiety Disorders.

GENERALISED ANXIETY DISORDER

Generalised Anxiety Disorder (GAD) is characterised by persistent, generalised and excessive feelings of anxiety which occur without any particular environmental circumstances, and caused by a general tendency to worry excessively. Typical worries including, exaggerated and excessive concerns about the 'possibility' of a negative situation occurring for example, a family member becoming ill or having an accident, performing poorly at work or socially. The symptoms will affect you in that you may have a problem with making daily decisions and remembering commitments as a result of a lack of concentration and preoccupation with worry.

The checklist below is designed to help you reflect on your situation or that of someone close to you, and not to provide a diagnosis - for that it is recommended that you see a doctor who will be able to tell you if you have symptoms in common with people who suffer from GAD.

You must have been bothered by these common symptoms of Generalised Anxiety Disorder on most days for a period of at least several weeks, but usually for a period of 6 months:

- Nervousness or restlessness
- Trembling
- Trouble falling or staying asleep
- Sweating
- Poor concentration
- Palpitations
- Frequent urination
- Muscular tension
- Easily fatigued
- Irritable mood
- Light-headedness or dizziness
- Hypervigilance
- Shortness of breath
- Depressed mood

PANIC DISORDER

In panic disorder, a person suffers from brief attacks of intense fear and apprehension, often characterised by trembling, shaking, confusion, dizziness, nausea, difficulty breathing. These panic attacks or anxiety attacks, as they are also known, are described as fear or discomfort that abruptly arises and peaks in less than ten minutes, can last for several hours and, can be triggered by stress, fear, or even exercise.

Common symptoms of a panic attack include:

- Shortness of breath
- Dizziness or light-headedness
- Tightness or pain in the chest
- Faintness
- Trembling or shaking
- Feelings of unreality
- Dry mouth
- Muscle tension
- Difficulty gathering thoughts or speaking
- Pounding heart
- Tingling fingers or feet
- A choking or smothering feeling
- Sweating
- Hot or cold flushes
- Urge to flee
- Nausea or 'butterflies'
- Blurred vision
- Fear of dying, losing control, or going crazy

For a diagnosis of a Panic Disorder, the said attacks must have chronic consequences: either worry over the attacks' potential implications (being socially humiliated, losing control/going mad, or concerns related to physical health), persistent fear of future attacks, or significant changes in behaviour related to the attacks. Accordingly, those suffering from panic disorder experience symptoms even outside specific panic episodes. Often, symptoms can be so frightening that even the fear of having an anxiety attack can actually trigger one.

In some cases, a heightened awareness (hyper-vigilance) of body functioning can occur during a panic attack, wherein any perceived physiological change is interpreted as a possible life-threatening illness. Being hyper-vigilant about having a panic attack can often be a trigger to experiencing a panic attack. If a person experiences an unexpected panic attack they are highly likely to have substantial anxiety over the possibility of having another attack, and will fear and avoid whatever situation they believe may have induced that panic attack. In some cases, this fear may be so intense that in order to prevent a panic attack they may never or rarely leave their home. When this occurs the diagnosis of Panic Disorder with Agoraphobia can be made. Some of the symptoms of a panic attack can resemble that of a heart attack (eg., chest pain or tightness in the chest), so it is understandable and common for a person who is having a panic attack to think that they are having a heart attack. If chest pain is recurrent or long-lasting it is recommended that you seek immediate medical assistance and have a thorough medical assessment. If heart disease is not present following a medical assessment by your doctor, he/she should be able to tell you whether that subsequent chest pain is a result of anxiety or some other condition that might need to be further investigated. The information on the next page may be helpful for distinguishing between symptoms of panic and symptoms of a heart attack. Confirmation by your doctor is recommended as this is a guide only.

DISTINGUISHING A PANIC ATTACK FROM A HEART ATTACK

Symptoms	Heart Attack	Panic Attack
Pain	• May or not be present. • If present, the pain is often described as a 'crushing feeling' – like someone standing on the chest. • The pain is usually located in the center of the chest and may spread to the left arm, neck and back. • Pain is not usually made worse by breathing or by pressing on the chest. • Pain is usually persisting and lasts longer than 5 – 10 minutes.	• Any pain is usually described as 'sharp'. • The pain tends to be localised over the heart. • Pain is usually made worse by breathing in and out and by pressing on the center of the chest. • Pain usually disappears within about 5-10 minutes.
Tingling	• Tingling is usually in the left arm.	• Tingling is usually present all over the body.
Vomiting	• Common	• Nausea may be present but vomiting is less common.
Breathing	• A heart attack does not cause you to hyperventilate – panic does. • With a heart attack you may feel a little short of breath. It is possible, however, to have a heart attack and then start panicking. In this case, hyperventilation is a symptom of panic, not of the heart attack.	• Hyperventilation is an extremely common panic response which precedes most panic attacks.

(World Health Organisation Collaborating Centre for Evidence in Mental Health Policy, 2000).

THE NATURE OF ANXIETY

Anxiety is a normal and healthy necessary response to deal with threat or danger very quickly. Threatening situations such as, being involved in a motor vehicle accident, being chased by a dog, cause physical, mental and behavioural changes to occur automatically in the body. These changes are caused by hormones that are released by the brain.

Once the brain becomes aware of danger and hormones are released, the involuntary nervous system then sends signals to various parts of the body to prepare us for the 'flight or fight' response. The following 'normal' changes to the body occur in response to these hormones, in particular Adrenalin;

Symptoms associated with the Fight-or-Flight Response:

- The mind becomes alert
- Blood clotting ability increases, preparing for possible injury
- Heart rate speeds up and blood pressure rises
- Sweating increases to help cool the body
- Blood is diverted to the muscles which tense ready for action
- Digestion slows down
- Saliva production decreases causing a dry mouth
- Breathing rate speeds up
- Liver releases sugar to provide quick energy
- Immune responses decrease
- Fear and apprehension
- Trembling or shaking
- Restlessness
- Cold and clammy hands
- Hot flushes or chills
- Feeling sick or nauseous
- Butterflies in the stomach

These symptoms are 'normal' and useful in coping with a realistic fear. The more alert, flexible, strong, fast, agile, and powerful we are the more capable we are of handling a difficult situation.

The 'Fight or Flight' response is useful in the short-term to deal with physical dangers but not in the long-term for most 21st century stressful situations such as, being pulled over by the police for speeding, or being threatened by the boss. Normally when the brain interprets a threatening situation, it will release the required amount of adrenalin to deal with that situation. If the threat is 'misinterpreted' as being worse than it really is, an excess amount of adrenalin will be released. Once the degree of threat is put into perspective, because this excess adrenalin is not required the symptoms must be waited out. Fighting the symptoms will result in prolonging the waiting period which usually lasts less than 10 minutes.

Most suffers of Panic Attacks exaggerate the level of fear or the degree of implication of a realistic fear. According to World Health Organisation, with the correct professional help 70%–90% of those suffering from panic disorder are helped in 6–8 weeks. Psycho-education, particularly about the nature of a Panic Disorder is the first step in managing this condition. However, treatment should focus not only on managing panic attacks but also on prevention. Prevention means identifying the cause which is usually, unwarranted excessive worrying, or in the case of panic disorders, worrying about having a panic attack.

SUSCEPTIBILITY TO MENTAL ILLNESS

So why are some people more susceptible to developing a mental illness than others? What are the missing ingredient/s? Researchers have identified a number of contributing factors including, chemical imbalances, situational or environmental factors, genetics and personality. Depression for instance is said to be caused by an imbalance of chemicals in the brain called neurotransmitters, including **serotonin**, **norepinephrine**, and **dopamine**, the neurotransmitters necessary to regulate emotions and mood. Studies have found that situational or **environmental factors** also seem to play a role in the onset or relapse of Depression. These include traumas or stressors, such as the loss of a loved one, loss of a job, or a divorce. Depression may also run in families. Current research is searching for specific genes that may be involved in passing a tendency toward developing depression in family lines. Personality traits are also considered to be an important factor.

Despite the lack of conclusive evidence about the exact cause of Depression, research indicates that Depression is a genetic and biological disorder that is affected by life stress and personality style. While there has been a lot of emphasis on how these factors control and affect us, there appears to be little emphasis on, 'what regulates our neurotransmitters, that are critical in regulating our emotions and moods that affect our behaviours and physical reactions. So if neurotransmitters are responsible for regulating our emotions then what controls the release of appropriate levels of neurotransmitters? The Mind. Our mind is the operator, our brain the engine, and our body is the vehicle. Our mind and how we think and interpret situations controls the chemicals released by our brain and these chemicals control our emotions and behaviour.

Based on my clinical experience in treating people with mental illness, the key to overcoming psychological conditions such as, Depression and Anxiety is to treat at the cognition level rather than the emotion or physical level. How you think – regulates how you feel. Thinking negatively ("what if?") will release the hormones (neurotransmitters) that create the negative emotion (fear). That negative emotion will then result in a negative reaction (anxiety). For instance,

> *If you believe that you will not successfully get that job, your brain will release the relevant hormones required to prepare you for a negative outcome. You will feel less enthusiastic, weary, apprehensive, down or even anxious. You will then experience physical symptoms, upset stomach, or racing heart, shallow and fast breathing, tensed muscles, or nauseous.*

Changing the way that we think about situations is the key to changing the way we feel. In saying that, this does not mean that feeling negative is always a bad thing. It is only a 'bad thing' when there is no justification for that negative emotion – this is known as 'catastrophic thinking' or 'irrational thinking'. When there is justification for that negative emotion, the brain will release the necessary neurotransmitters required to deal with the actual threat appropriately. Your body requires these hormones for strength, speed, agility and alertness.

People who suffer from Depression or Anxiety have a tendency to have patterns of irrational thoughts, catastrophic thinking and distorted beliefs. This causes them to live with constant fear and avoid situations that create that fear. They live a very guarded life within their comfort zone. As a result, they will often feel ***trapped, lost and not in control*** of their life. The blog below is a typical example of how most people feel when suffering from symptoms of Depression and/or Anxiety:

> *Things that I really want to do: to get a new job and to start meeting new people with the goal of eventually finding a relationship. I'm scared of committing to anything, relationships, studying etc. in case I get hurt or put effort in and fail or discover the effort wasn't worth it in the end. I want these things so badly, but I am so afraid of letting go and actually taking the risk, I'm so comfortable with the current state, I feel safe. What's the risk? What is really at risk here? Failure. I want to do something with my life but what's the point of initial success and eventual failure? I hardly ever put the necessary effort in anything, which has led to dissatisfaction throughout my entire life. It's easier to just quit or give up. Why am I afraid of success? I am going to be thirty-two in three weeks. I feel that I have wasted my life away. I really don't want to look back at my life and say that it was a lifetime of no effort, that's too depressing for words. If that's true, then, no matter what, I have to keep on trying. Better to see what doing something will lead to than doing nothing. Waiting without action only leads to nothing, not even a dead end. How do you change a lifetime habit? How do you completely change everything you don't like about yourself? I read of people reinventing themselves. How do they do that? I'm really determined to change my ways... i want to try, and live a full life without always being anxious. I want to enjoy things not always worry about what might happen and the future. I have to keep trying.*
>
> *Blog – Phillip. D – Queensland.*

Irrational Thinking and irrational beliefs will result in ***Fear.***

Fear will result in ***Avoidance.***

Avoidance will result in feeling ***Trapped and Lost.***

Feeling trapped and lost will result in feeling, ***Unhappy and an Unfulfilled life –hence Depression.***

CHAPTER TWO

CONTROLLED BY FEAR

"The other side of every fear is freedom"

EMOTIONS play a very functional role in our daily lives. Our emotions motivate us, drive our appraisal of situations, and in some cases can have consequential effects on our behaviour in response to those situations. Competent emotional functioning is fundamental in the development of healthy social relationships, higher self-esteem and life satisfaction, and in the prevention of mental disorders. There is sufficient research indicating that poor emotional functioning is implicated in more than half of the mental disorders included in the Diagnostic and Statistical Manual of Mental Disorders, and predictive of poorer social competence and peer acceptance. Therefore, controlling our emotions and responding to a situation in an appropriate and effective manner is vital to our well-being. Even negative emotions such as fear, when regulated can play a vital role in our lives.

Fear is an important and valuable emotion. It warns us about danger and activates a coping response to a perceived threat. It is an appropriate response as an adaptive function to particular events or actual threats. We are designed to survive emergencies. Suppose for instance, that we meet a tiger on the road. What happens? We perceive an actual threat (Cognition) – the adrenal gland releases Adrenalin (Hormone) – a moderate level of anxiety is experienced – and we experience Fear (Emotion). Adrenalin, also known as Epinephrine, is a hormone and neurotransmitter that activates the fight or flight mechanism in our brain and body. It is the fuel behind a lot of the symptoms and sensations that we endure during anxiety. Once our brain receives a message that we are in trouble, adrenalin is pumped into our bloodstream and causes our heart rate to increase (to increase oxygen), dilates pupils (for better vision), increases sweat production (to keep us cool in case we need to run), suppresses immune system (as it is not needed in dangerous situations), blood clotting ability increases (in case of an injury), the liver releases sugar (to provide quick energy), and creates a general (but awful) feeling of fear.

This reaction is supposed to help us survive a potentially life threatening situation. But what if most of the time our reaction is a false alarm and even though we feel like we are ready for action, there is nothing going on.

If adrenalin is moderately high for a long period of time, we will feel anxious and wonder why. This is called "free-floating", anxiety. If, on the other hand, Adrenalin shoots up to a very high level rapidly, and then decreases rapidly (approximately 5 to 10 minutes), and the anxiety is brief but intense - this is called a "panic attack". If we regularly associate a particular 'thing' to the anxiety, such as heights or spiders, that's called a "phobia".

So how does anxiety become a problem? The human body has a self-adjusting system, called ADAPTATION. If we repeatedly have false alarms the body learns to dump larger and larger amounts of adrenalin at the slightest hint of an emergency. The adrenal gland doesn't just put out adrenalin, but about 60 different hormones. Repeated dumps of adrenalin will affect all the other hormones in our body. This will contribute to hormone imbalances. Fear is only useful if it protects us from real threats, and the level of adrenalin released is in proportion to that danger. Unrealistic or irrational fear is one of the major contributing factors to the development of Anxiety Disorders including Panic Disorder and Generalised Anxiety Disorder. Irrational fear is the habit of worrying only on the 'possibilities' of something happening without taking into consideration the 'probabilities' of it happening. Alternatively, 'rational fear' is the ability to accurately calculate risk and avoid consequence – it is a form of good judgement. Fear is only helpful when it is controlled not when it controls us.

So how do we allow Fear to control us?

EMOTION REGULATION

Emotion Regulation involves recognising, monitoring, evaluating and modifying emotional responses in accordance to situations. By learning to manage our emotions we should be able to decrease the intensity and frequency of our emotional states.

According to research findings, both personality and perceived parenting behaviours are predictable factors in the development of **appropriate emotion regulation**. Parental care appears to be a significant predictor in functional emotional regulation. The presence or lack of a nurturing and supportive care-giving environment is of particular importance for a child's functional emotional regulation development. Therefore, growing up experiencing positive parental response is more likely to develop secure attachment. Growing up with a parent validating your negative emotions by telling you "it's ok to feel this way and coaching you on how to regulate your emotions is important in the development of secure attachment and appropriate emotion regulation techniques. The quality of parent-child interactions forms the basis of the attachment relationship and this has been found to have profound implications on a child's experience, expression and regulation of an emotion. Securely attached children openly express and share their emotions.

> *So if a parent tells their child that they had the right to be upset by a comment made by a fellow student (validate the emotion), and then coached them on how to express that emotion appropriately (regulate the emotion), that child is more likely to cope better with negative situations in the future.*

On the other-hand –

> *If a child is told to toughen up and condemned for expressing their feelings, they are more likely to learn to suppress their emotions in an attempt to minimise their potential rejection from others and less likely to cope with negative situations in the future.*

People who learn to regulate their emotions are more likely to negotiate stressful events by interpreting them in a more optimistic way, and more likely to experience and express more positive affect and less negative affect. Regulating emotions appropriately requires both emotion validation and emotion expression. Believing you have the right to experience that emotion and the right to express that emotion appropriately is – Emotion Regulation.

Therefore, controlling emotional states by accurately appraising a negative eliciting situation is a necessary step in expressing justified emotions appropriately. The difficulty lies in the ability to appraise a negative situation accurately in order to express the appropriate emotion required for that situation.

One of the most debilitating of all emotions is **unjustified fear** - fear that is unwarranted and exaggerated. How many times have you over-reacted to the "What if?" question only to find that what you expected to happen never did? This occurs as a result of a lack of appraisal of the potential anxiety-provoking situation. Living constantly with irrational fear is not only physically debilitating, but also psychologically impairing. If fear starts to control you, or prevent you from taking any risks, then it becomes a handicap. People who suffer from a mental illness such as, Anxiety Disorder or Depression are controlled by irrational fear and this fear can affect every aspect of their life. When unwarranted fear is experienced, the anxiety symptoms experienced are real, but the situation that elicits this irrational fear is not. The expected consequence from that situation is either exaggerated or the situation expected does not even occur. Nevertheless, the fear and its affect are so distressing that we are compelled to avoid potential anxiety-provoking situations.

People who rely on Avoidance as a coping mechanism usually have a fear of living life and cannot live their potential. They might have a fear of making a mistake, fear of rejection, fear of failure, fear of being judged or criticised by others, fear of commitment, fear of conflict or of confrontation, fear of taking risks and of stepping out of their comfort zone, fear of making decisions, fear of sharing their opinions or disagreeing, fear of asking for help, fear of meeting their own needs and rights – and fear of being themselves. This fear is usually unjustified and irrational. Avoiding fear can have a detrimental effect on our psychological state, our relationships, and on the way we live our life.

AVOIDING FEAR

The human system is conditioned to seek 'positive experiences' that create 'positive feelings', and avoid 'negative experiences', that evoke 'negative feelings'. We see this in our children when they avoid their chores because "that's boring", and yet cannot take them away from chatting to their friends online, because "that's exciting". So, when we expect a situation to cause anxiety we do everything possible to avoid it. Avoiding the challenging opportunities offered throughout our life not only prevents potential growth, but also creates an unstimulating and unsatisfactory life.

Staying within our comfort zone to avoid anxiety can only lead to feeling trapped and unfulfilled.

If you want to audition for a part in the local play and the thought of embarrassing yourself or of being rejected creates anxiety, avoiding that opportunity will not only prevent you from meeting your potential but also force you to stay in an area you have outgrown and therefore no longer stimulating.

I see a lot of cases in my practice of people suffering from Depression and/or Anxiety who report feeling 'lost and trapped' in their life, and they report not having formed an identity of their own. They are too frightened to step out of their comfort zone and take on any opportunity that they are presented with such as, a new job opportunity, a friendship, a promotion, a business opportunity, commitment to a relationship, and/or starting a new family etc. They will report not feeling content or fulfilled or comfortable in the following areas of their life:

- **Family Life** (Immediate, Extended Family)
- **Personal Relationships** (Friendships, Partners)
- **Work Life** (Training, Voluntary work, Paid Employment, Projects)
- **Social Life** (Social groups)
- **Recreational Life** (Relaxation Activities, Hobbies)

In my practice, it is not uncommon to hear clients who suffer from Depression or Anxiety report that they feel satisfied only with one or two of these areas in their life. The most common barriers to achieving a more fulfilling life are fear of failure and a fear of rejection.

FAMILY LIFE

In their Family and Personal Relationships, they feel obligated to overplease, over-commit and don't feel that their relationships have open and honest communication and they feel they can't be themselves or be genuine. They fear rejection, conflict, and of being criticised or judged.

"I won't tell him how I really feel because it might lead to a conflict"

"If I don't help them shift their house, I will lose them as friends"

"I can't join the Bridge Club because I have to babysit my grandchild"

"I wish I can tell him how his comment hurt my feelings, it made me feel stupid"

WORK LIFE

In their Work Life, they feel compelled to staying in a job that they are familiar with and feel 'safe' rather than taking a risk and doing the job they really 'want'. It's a job that they have mastered and the risk of making a mistake is zero. They feel unstimulated, and discouraged at seeing everyone around them being promoted. They don't want to take the risk, just in case they fail.

"It made me feel good the boss offering me the promotion, but if I take it and fail, I'll feel embarrassed and he'll see my weaknesses"

"My wife keeps pushing me to get a better paying job, I can't tell her I'm not confident with change".

SOCIAL LIFE

In their Social Life, they don't feel like they 'fit in', they sit back and observe others interacting rather than participating just in case, they say something stupid, or can't communicate their point across properly. They fear being rejected, excluded, or judged. They believe it's easier to not socialise then to set themselves up and get hurt by the rejection as this would only confirm to them how worthless they believe they are.

"I don't enjoy meeting with the group, I never know what to wear"

"I feel stupid just saying nothing they must think there's something wrong with me"

"If I say something it might come out wrong"

RECREATIONAL LIFE

In their Recreational Life, they fear failure and of commitment. They worry about discovering that they are not good at a particular task so they don't try at all. They worry about committing to an activity that will continuously demonstrate their incompetence to others and to themselves.

"What if I'm not good at soccer and can't just quit"

"What if I'm the only one in the class who can't paint?"

"I don't want to spend all that money on golf, what if I'm bad at it?"

It is easy to see how irrational fear can have a significant effect on every aspect of our life. And how staying within our comfort zone can prevent us from developing a sense of belonging, sense of purpose, sense of achievement, and a stimulating and fulfilling life.

STEPPING OUT OF OUR COMFORT ZONE

So what happens if we are forced out of our comfort zone? For example, how would we feel if the boss suddenly told us that we are to be in charge of the division while he was away on a trip? – If we are prone to suffering anxiety then we would initially feel like we have been thrown into the deep end – but we would eventually work out that we can actually swim – and get the job done regardless of how 'uncomfortable and scary' the journey was. Being forced out of our comfort zone can result in building confidence in that particular situation/activity but the next time we are 'thrown' into another situation, unless it is exactly the same as or similar to the previous situation, we are likely to experience the same degree of anxiety. Why? because the trigger to the anxiety (irrational fear of failure) has not been addressed and we have only developed confidence in that specific situation by becoming desensitised to it.

Unfortunately, it is not always possible to avoid challenging and stressful situations that provoke anxiety. Being forced out of our comfort zone and having to experience anxiety provoking situations can be an exhausting and frightening experience. The amount of adrenalin dispensed to cope with these situations will leave us feeling 'depleted'.

Often there is an internal conflict between wanting to escape the feelings of anxiety induced by stepping out of our comfort zone, and wanting to escape the feelings of worthlessness induced by staying within our comfort zone. Basically, we are damned if we do (by suffering anxiety), and damned if we don't (by suffering depression). Can you see the link between avoidance and Depression?

Excessive stress for long periods of time can also contribute to the development of Depression. While some stressful situations cannot be avoided or controlled, in a lot of cases, the most common cause is poor stress management skills rather than the situation itself.

STRESS AND DEPRESSION

Stress can occur as a result of an imbalance between demands and resources. Not feeling in control of an event can lead to stress. Often ineffective stress management skills can contribute to the inability to control a stressful event.

Life stressors such as, death of a loved one, personal illness, divorce, loss of a job, financial difficulties, or major changes such as, new baby, moving house et cetera, are all risk factors that can be extremely disruptive on mental health. Two people can experience the same risk factor, and one may experience a depressive episode while the other may not. Stress management skills or lack of, affects an individual's risk of depression. Effective stress management skills enable us to cope with the stressor, and to move forward. For instance:

> *If you became unemployed and saw this as an opportunity for a career change or to find a better job, then you would accept this loss a lot easily.*

On the other-hand,

> *If you personalised the loss of your job and believed that your chances of finding another job was low, then you would find it difficult to adapt to and accept the job loss and this may trigger an episode of depression.*

Effective stress management involve; proactive problem-solving, assertiveness skills, conflict-resolution skills, and a healthy self-esteem. When we have healthy stress management skills, we are more likely to experience 'normal ups and downs' when faced with positive and negative events.

People who experience recurrent episodes of Depression are unlikely to experience normal 'ups and downs' and are more likely instead to experience at their best, symptoms of 'mild to moderate' depression. Because symptoms are not as debilitating at the mild to moderate level as they are at the moderate to severe level, depression is often left undetected and unfortunately untreated. This is why it is more common for people to seek therapy when they are at the 'moderate to severe' range of Depression as this is the stage that they are likely to function the less.

An episode of depression will often be triggered by a stressful or challenging life event that the person has not been able to cope with and therefore, proactively deal with. These triggers will often force them from a mild level into a severe level of depression which can last weeks, months and even years. These severe episodes eventually decrease to mild levels usually once the stressor has resolved, or as soon as a positive event has occurred such as, obtaining a new job, new relationship or something positive. However, without healthy stress management skills, unfortunately, dropping to mild levels of depression can be the best that some sufferers of depression can ever experience.

Diagram 2.1 demonstrates the pattern of healthy stress management. l) a stressor is immediately and appropriately dealt with, 2) the person enters the 'recovery' stage which continues until the next stressor arises 3) that stressor is then dealt with, and 4) the person enters the 'recovery' stage and so on.

Diagram 2.2 demonstrates the pattern of unhealthy stress management. 1) As each stressor arises and not dealt with, a 'snowballing' effect occurs and the person is forced to remain above their stress threshold. 2) If this occurs for too long a period, the person will enter the 'exhaustion' stage, and this can trigger an episode of depression.

DIAGRAM 2.1

Stress/Depression

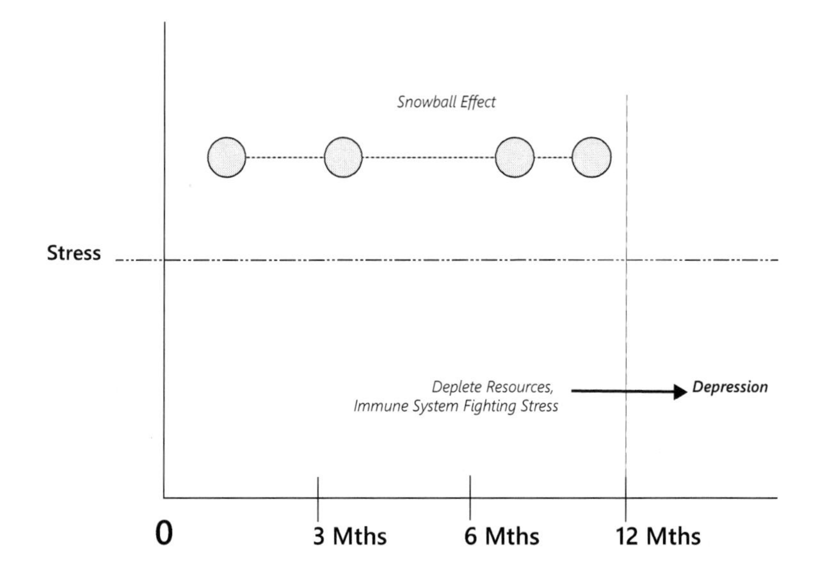

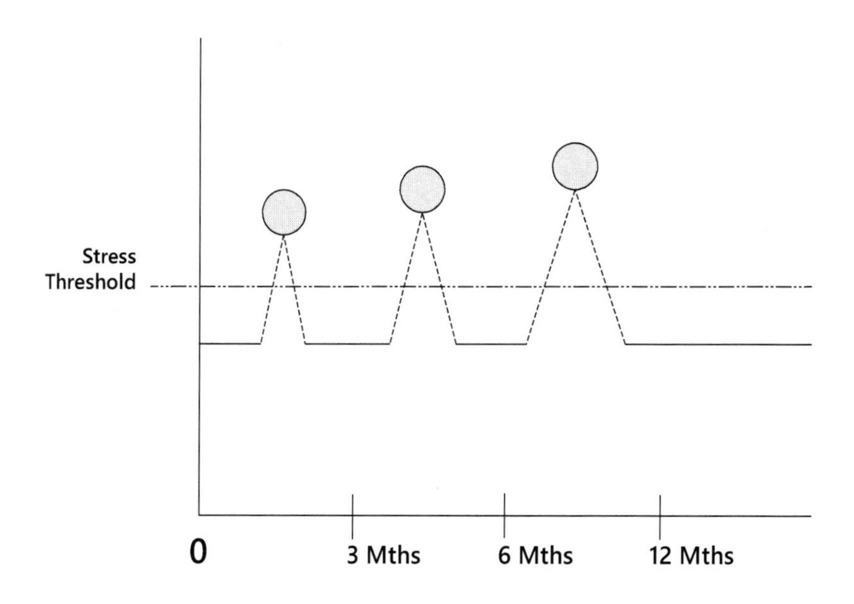

Diagram 2.2 demonstrates the different levels someone who is susceptible to depression falls into as a result of the stressors experienced at different stages in their life – hence 'recurrent episodes of depression'.

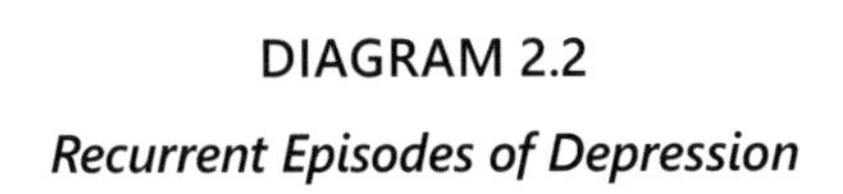

DIAGRAM 2.2

Recurrent Episodes of Depression

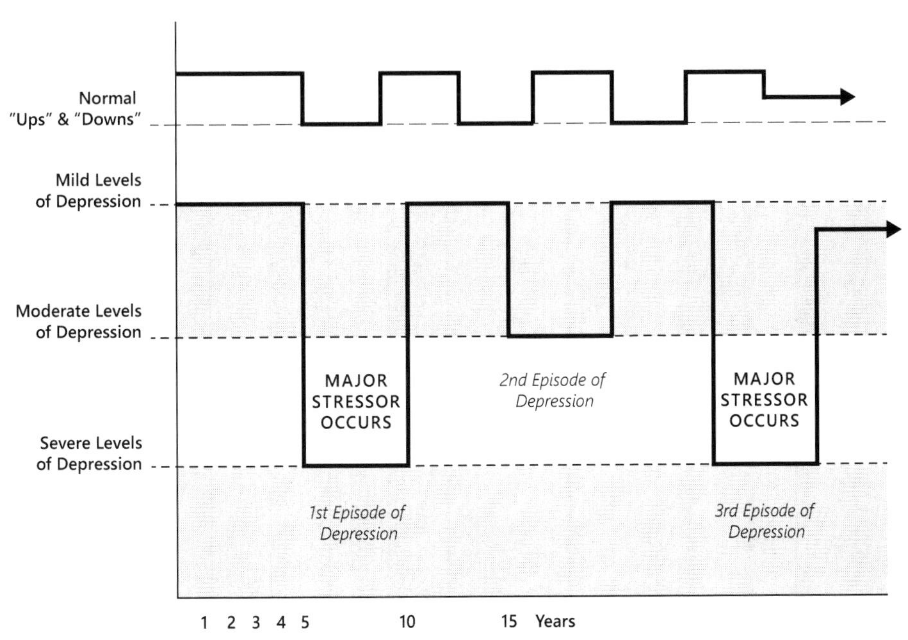

While it would be ideal, it is not always possible to escape life's stressors and challenges – furthermore, these life challenges play an important role in growth – hence the need for effective stress management skills. People who do not cope with life stressors usually do not apply effective stress management skills, and have a high tendency to avoid difficult people and situations, over-react to these situations rather than take a proactive 'solution-focused' approach, and have very little faith in their abilities to deal with a challenging situation or difficult person due to low self-esteem. In most cases, it is poor perception of their capabilities in dealing with potentially negative situations and not a lack of the necessary skills that is the barrier to dealing with these situations effectively and proactively.

Irrational/unrealistic fear of dealing with challenging people and situation, and of interacting with others, and the external environment, will result in an unfulfilled, dissatisfied and unhappy life.

So irrational fear not only controls the way we deal with life stressors, but also the choices we make that affect the quality of our lives and relationships.

How do we develop irrational fear? If the key to change is to let go of fear, then how do we control it so that it no longer has control over us?

CHAPTER THREE

IRRATIONAL FEAR

"UNREALISTIC FEAR – False Evidence Appearing Real"

SO, why are some people controlled by irrational fear and not others? Why are some people better able to rationalise their fear than others? And how can it be controlled?

Why, are some people more affected than others when they make a mistake, or when they fail at something or when they are criticised by others? How many times have you noticed someone make a mistake and just shrug it off – and wonder why you can't do the same? The answer is – how they interpret the situation. It is how they assess that outcome in terms of its degree of severity and the consequence they expect from that outcome that enables them to do this. Basically, they have the right formula to regulate their emotion and response to that situation. *They interpreted the situation as being a minor problem and have therefore, reacted to that problem appropriately.* That does not mean that they did not experience a negative emotion from that situation, they may have experienced annoyance, or frustration at having to *fix up their mistake* – but they did not 'overreact' or experience an 'exaggerated emotion' such as, fear, anger or melancholy.

So, why do some people overreact to a similar situation?" Their interpretation of not only what that *mistake* symbolises for them, but also the consequence they expect that *mistake* to cost them will contribute to their emotional reaction. If they interpreted their mistake to mean that they are not *a smart person* and expect their employer to think that they are not the right person for the job for having made that mistake – then they are likely to experience an 'exaggerated emotion' such as, fear, depressed moods, or anger. Therefore, how we evaluate situations significantly influences how we will feel and respond to that situation. How we think regulates how we feel and how we feel regulates how we behaviour.

So, what is the key to regulating our emotions?

OUR PERCEPTIONS INFLUENCE OUR EMOTIONS AND ATTITUDES

The key to controlling emotion such as fear is to stay in the rational realm by mastering the method of accurately interpreting what you perceive.

The process of attaching a meaning to what is perceived is crucial in the construction of personal and social reality? – This is called Perception.

Our eyes, ears, nose, tongue and skin are the receptors for the sensations in our body – (sight, hearing, taste and smell). Therefore, a sensation is a response to something. For example, the baby's eyes (receptor) enables it to see (sense) the toy. The baby doesn't need to understand what that toy is, to see that it is there.

In psychology, **Perception** is the process of attaining awareness or understanding of sensory information. So, when the baby sees the toy and through repeated experiences, learns that it is a toy, "the sensation has moved on to perception". A small child with no experience of 'hot' who sees a bright stove element or a lit candle may be attracted to the visual stimulus and touch it, and through the immediate painful sensation felt in its hand, learns about 'hot'. That learning involved the transition from Sensation to Perception. The child has attached the meaning 'hot' to the object 'stove'. So, our emotion and behaviour is influenced by the meaning we attach to the object or situation.

If we attach a negative meaning to a situation or object, then we will respond to that with a negative emotion such as, fear, anger, sadness or frustration. On the other hand, if we attach a positive meaning we will react and feel in a positive way. Our sensory, perception, emotions, and behaviour are designed to work collaboratively. If our perception is not in sync with reality, then our emotions will also not be in sync, and neither will our response to the perceived situation. While we are born with the ability to sense, perception is an active process that is developed from the experiences we encountered throughout our life since birth. It involves learning and understanding ourselves, others and the world and as such, essential in the development of human relations and our well-being.

If perception is the tap that regulates our emotion, and our emotion is the tap to regulating our behaviour and attitudes, then it is critical that our perception of situations is accurate. So, if perception is something that can be learned, then what causes perceptual errors? Why are some people able to perceive situations more accurately then others? What influences our perception?

OUR BELIEFS INFLUENCE OUR PERCEPTIONS

What you perceive is a result of interplays between (a) past experiences, including cultural influences (the mental maps we have constructed from past experiences), and (b) the technique we use to evaluate the perceived stimuli. Since the day we were born, our brain has been receiving and storing information from anyone that ever exerted (or still exert) any influence on us from the (socio-cultural economic) environment in which we grew up. From family or peer groups when we were younger or comments we received from our partner, teachers, parents, work colleagues, children, relatives, media, television and books. All the assumptions we made about life from both negative and positive experiences have shaped our core belief system.

Therefore, it is this core belief system that we use to understand what is happening around us. It is what we use to 'filter' the information we are continuously presented with, and the 'meaning' we give to this information. Hence, we see what we are conditioned to see.

Each person has their own unique perceptual filter consisting of the beliefs and values that they have collected and stored since the day they were born. These filters are the personal belief systems that we rely on to live our lives. Our beliefs, values and past experiences affect how we represent things in our mind. When situations are viewed without understanding, the mind will try to reach for something that it already recognises (from our past experiences) in order to process what it is viewing. Our beliefs define us in terms of who we are and what we can be or do, and our perception of how a situation will work out also depend on these beliefs. If our 'filter' consists of distorted beliefs, then our perception of new experiences will also be 'tainted', and we will respond accordingly. For example –

> *If we were repeatedly told by a significant person in childhood that we were 'useless and worthless', then we are likely to have this belief stored, and this belief may be preventing us from taking that promotion, or enrolling in that course, or committing to that relationship, even though that belief may be inaccurate.*

Whatever we do or don't do in any given situation is the direct result of what and how we perceive the situation, and the beliefs we refer to. Our beliefs influence how we perceive a situation and this perception influences the way we behave and interact in certain situations. For example -

> *If a waiter has the core belief that "customers deserve good service" then he will demonstrate this through his behaviour by being genuinely friendly, polite and diligent. However, if his core belief was that "people do not appreciate good service" then he is likely to be rude to customers and deliver poor service.*

Behaviour that is influenced by a distorted belief will reinforce that same belief. For example –

> *If you were continuously criticised as a child for making mistakes, you may have developed the belief that "mistakes results in a negative consequence", or that "you don't have the right to make a mistake" (Belief). You might then perceive that making a mistake in your new job "will cost you your job' (Perception), and then decide to quit your job (Action). This might then reinforce the belief, "I can't do anything right", or "I always make mistakes" or I'm not a quick learner"* ***(Reinforced Belief).***

If our belief is that 'we have poor social skills' - avoiding social opportunities will only reinforce this belief.

If we have the belief that 'we are not smart' – failing a subject will only reinforce that belief.

Beliefs therefore, serve as 'filters' that impact on our perception of situations, and our perceptions then influence our actions, and our actions then reinforce our beliefs. This ***Belief ► Perception ► Action ► Belief*** cycle will further impinge on our lives.

So the way we interact with the environment largely depends on the core belief system we have created. If the information stored is inaccurate it will limit us, if it is accurate, it will empower us. When our beliefs are accurate, our assessment of our relationships, ourselves, and of the world will also be accurate - hence our attitudes and emotions will also be appropriate. Beliefs proven to be rational and useful that accurately represent the external reality, can either take you where you want to go, or keep you where you are.

Although we are in control of what meaning we give a situation, that control largely depends on our core belief system. Cleaning out our 'filter' of distorted beliefs is a critical step in regaining control over our emotions, behaviour, and our life.

OUR PERCEPTIONS INFLUENCE OUR BELIEFS

While it is clear to see how our beliefs influence our perception of situations, so too can our perception have an effect on our belief system. As previously discussed, distorted beliefs will interfere with our interpretation of situations by **'clouding'** our objective judgement. However, our distorted 'filter' is not the only causal factor of perceptual errors, the technique in which we collect and evaluate the information required to make that 'objective judgement' must also be right. The experience alone can't provide absolute certainty, it is therefore important to be able to look to reasoning, and most importantly, that the method of reasoning is correct otherwise, this can result in the creation of irrational beliefs. For example -

> *If we have always been successful in our job for a number of years, and our position is suddenly made redundant, and we interpret the reason for the redundancy to be due to our poor performance, then we are likely to create a new belief. This belief whether accurate or not will be relied on to make predictions on future outcomes.*

Once we believe something to be true, we find it is extremely difficult to delete information that contradicts the belief. In fact, once we have a belief, we go through life searching for information that supports the belief and ignoring information that does not. In many cases, the external environment contains sufficient evidence to prove or disprove the belief we might have about a situation. Regardless of this, we will be more prone to collecting the evidence that supports the belief we believe to be true. For example –

> *If you believe that most people are bad you can find ample evidence in the news and from your experiences with people you encounter in your life to support that belief. On the other hand, if you believe that most people are good you will find plenty of evidence to support that belief as well.*

The fact is, events themselves don't have any power - it's the meaning and interpretation we give them that determines this. Two people can go through the same experience and depending on how that experience is interpreted, will come out of it with differing accounts.

Hence, our method of reasoning must be correct if we are to create accurate beliefs that we will store and retrieve to assess new experiences or to predict future outcomes. When accurate beliefs are stored in our mind, we are more likely to make accurate assessments of new situations and have a much more accurate prediction of outcomes, and this can only contribute to our well-being. Using the above example –

> *If we accurately evaluated and interpreted the reason behind the redundancy as being due to situational factors and not due to poor performance, then the belief we will maintain is that we are successful in our job. This healthy belief will continue to influence us in a positive way in the future.*

As you can see our perceptions are influenced by the beliefs and values we have created based on previous perceptions **(Perceptions ► Beliefs ► Perceptions)**. Our actions and emotions are determined by interpreting the event accurately, and by having an accurate core belief system, not by what is happening in our life. This formula can be learned. It is never too late to change our belief systems and perceptions. For some people making perceptual errors when evaluating situations has become an automatic unconscious process despite the fact that we have a choice in how we represent things to ourselves. Being aware of your own thoughts, beliefs and perceptions is the start to becoming more present with others and life in general. Learning the technique of rationally evaluating events, and identifying, recognising and correcting beliefs that limit you is also a crucial step that will be covered later on in this book.

There are many books that outline the necessary step in *changing how we think ('thinking more positively')* to change how we feel about and how we respond to situations. While it is true that *how you think* determines *how you feel*, it is not easy to correcting unhealthy patterns of thinking without changing the beliefs that negatively influence our cognitions. How many times have you tried 'thinking more positively', or 'relied on affirmations' only to find that although your mood has improved, it has not lasted?

Based on my clinical experience, I have found that the majority of people who suffer from Depression and Anxiety Disorders hold on to beliefs that may not be accurate and that have been reinforced overtime into their subconscious. These beliefs can replay over and over in their head in their daily self-talk, with or without their awareness and potentially sabotage their efforts.

Since our perceptions and beliefs govern how we feel about ourselves and how we behave, then it is crucial that we see ourselves for who we actually are – 'our true self'. A strong sense of self-worth and positive self-perception are two important keys to living a productive and enjoyable life. When we better understand ourselves and when we expand our self-image, we expand the possibilities. It will lead us to building better relationships with others and guide us in meeting our personal and/or professional life goals. On the other-hand if we have a negative perception of ourselves, then this will have a negative impact on how we think and how we expect things to work out. If you see yourself as worthless, hopeless, and useless, then you are likely to expect to fail at things, to be rejected by people, to make mistakes, to be criticised by others, to make the wrong decisions, to be blamed for negative outcomes, and to not be valued by others.

> *If you believe you are a boring person, you are likely to experience a lot of anxiety when you meet someone new because you are going to expect to be rejected by them.*
>
> *You are going to expect to be fired if you believe you don't have the capabilities of doing the job.*

Your perception of yourself controls every aspect of your life, your relationships, your work life, recreational life, and your social life.

> *If you believe you are not intelligent enough to study a university degree, then you are likely to not attempt that degree if you expect to fail.*
>
> *If you believe that you will fail at anything you attempt, then you will only do the things that you have already trialled and tested.*

Having a negative based self-perception means that you have a more negative opinion of yourself than objective indicators warrant. That is, your 'perceived self' does not match your 'true self'. So how do we develop an accurate opinion of ourselves? – by mastering the art of assessing what is happening around us objectively rather than by coming to a conclusion based solely on an assumption. This is how you develop a healthy sense of self-worth – and once, you develop a healthy self-esteem, only then will you achieve the life you desire.

CHAPTER FOUR

THE SELF-WORTH THEORY

"To be yourself in a world that is constantly trying to make you someone else is the greatest accomplishment."

WHILE Self-esteem is not the only determinant of happiness, it is one of the most important. We are not born with self-esteem. Building self-esteem involves consistent effort. It is crucial in maintaining mental and physical well-being. There is sufficient evidence to suggest that raising self-esteem reduces symptoms of depression, anxiety and stress, and improves relationships.

Self-esteem appears to contribute to:

- Depression
- Anxiety
- Stress
- Dysfunctional relationships
- Alcohol and drug abuse
- Addictions
- Eating disorders
- Poor communication (eg., non-assertive, aggressive, defensive or sarcastic styles).
- Dependency
- Sensitivity to criticism
- Social difficulties
- Poor performance/achievement
- Preoccupation with problems
- Status concern
- Self-esteem is an 'invisible handicap' and highly correlated to overall life satisfaction.

DEFINITION OF SELF-WORTH

Self-worth or **self-esteem** as it is sometimes referred as, is a term used to indicate a person's overall evaluation or appraisal of their own worth as an individual person. It is their opinion of themselves – beliefs (for example, "I am competent", "I am valued") and the emotions (for example, "pride, guilt, disappointment) that they have about themselves.

When you have high self-esteem, you feel confident and competent in dealing with life's challenges, you feel able, right, and secure. However, when you have low self-worth you feel useless, not ready for life, and you do not feel right as a person. You do not feel on an equal plane with others.

People with a healthy level of self-esteem:

1. Stand firmly by the values and principles that they believe in, even when these are challenged by others.
2. Trust their own judgment and act on what they believe to be the best choice, even though others do not like them.
3. Do not worry excessively about the past or future and as such, are able to live in the present.
4. Believe in their capacity to solve problems, and feel comfortable to ask others for help when they need it.
5. Feel equal and not inferior or superior to others, and accepting individual differences in certain skills, personality, values, and beliefs.
6. Seek friendships and relationships that make them feel valued, respected, and that are positive and supportive.
7. Resist manipulation and only work with others if it is appropriate and convenient.
8. Are able to enjoy a vast variety of activities without apprehension.
9. Are sensitive to and respect other people's feelings and needs, and comfortable in setting boundaries.
10. They are able to stand up for their rights.
11. They are able to learn from their mistakes.
12. Are able to listen to other's point of views.
13. Take responsibility for their lives.
14. Have a sense of purpose and direction in their life.

People who suffers from low levels of self-esteem:

1. Constantly criticise themselves.
2. Are hypersensitive to criticism.
3. Have chronic difficulties in making decisions due a fear of making mistakes.
4. Over-please and over-commit to other's needs.
5. Have great difficulties in saying 'no' and in setting boundaries in relationships.
6. Have chronic self-blame.
7. Have high unrealistic expectations of themselves.

8. Constantly feel guilty over many things.
9. Are chronically pessimistic.
10. Have a constant fear of failure, rejection, and criticism.
11. Find it hard to enjoy any activity due to constant apprehension.
12. Believe they have more weaknesses than strengths.
13. Feel inferior to others.
14. Feel useless and worthless.
15. Do not believe they are able to do things as well as others.
16. Have no sense of purpose.

BEHAVIORAL SYMPTOMS OF LOW SELF-ESTEEM

- **Being Needy:** Low Self-Esteem Suffers will try harder to please in order to win the love, acceptance and attention of others.

- **Difficulties developing and maintaining relationships:** Being self-focused, hypersensitive, insecure, unreasonable expectations, holding in feelings, poor communication, misunderstandings, defensive are typical symptoms of low self-esteem. These behaviours will often interfere with building and maintaining close, honest and genuine relationships.

- **Defensive:** They become defensive even when given constructive criticism and will often deny the obvious, unable to admit a mistake, and have poor judgement.

- **Eating Disorders:** Eating disorders or unhealthy eating habits, such as, emotional eating is a typical symptom of Low Self-Esteem.

- **Hypervigilance:** Constantly anxious and fearful of making a mistake, they may search for signs on how to act, what to wear, what to say and what to do. They also frequently misinterpret what they see or hear often coming to an inaccurate conclusion.

- **Lack of assertiveness or have passive, aggressive, or passive-aggressive behavior, or poor communication.** They are often too fearful of being rejected by others, to tell the truth, ask for what they want, or share their feelings. People with Low Self-Esteem may also behave passive-aggressively when negative emotions build up and they can no longer contain them.

- **Perfectionism:** They feel imperfect, inadequate, and therefore, put tremendous energy into looking and acting in ways that are acceptable. For example, they may focus on always being the best dressed, needing to have perfect grades, or being the perfect parent. They think in terms of two extremes, black and white or all or nothing, success or failure, and anything less than perfection is considered a failure.

- **Set Poor Boundaries:** People who suffer from low self-esteem often tolerate the inappropriate behavior of others.

- **Poor Relationship and Social Skills:** They find themselves paralysed by not knowing what to say or do in social situations. They may dominate conversations in an attempt to fit in, feeling that others may find them not interesting enough they may sit back and not contributing to conversations.

- **Self-sabotaging:** Unable or unwilling to make changes, they take what comes their way. Fearful of failure or rejection, they may stay in jobs with inadequate pay, poor or no benefits, or in unhealthy and unfulfilling relationships.

- Because of anxiety and a lack of self-respect or appropriate skills, they **tend to rely on others** for decision-making, submit to others' ideas, values and ways to try and please. They can also become workaholics and overcommit, believing that success can bring them feelings of adequacy.

- **Mask their insecurities:** They feel that others will think less of them if they show emotion or let others see that they have problems or that they have difficulties in their lives.

For a more accurate assessment of your self-esteem I recommend Dr. Sorensen's "Sorensen Self-Esteem Test", **www.getesteem.com**.

Self-esteem is your sense of worth; your self-regard. It is your opinion of yourself; your self-evaluation.

SELF-WORTH, SELF-CONFIDENCE & SOCIAL-CONFIDENCE

Many people use the words self-esteem and self-confidence as if they mean the same thing. Self-esteem and self-confidence might be linked but they are, different. In fact, self-esteem is the broader category and self-confidence is one of its sub-categories. Self-esteem refers to our overall opinion of our self – our sense of personal worth in comparison to others. For example, feeing worthy, valued, and equal to others. Self-confidence on the other hand is our sense of accomplishment of particular tasks – our belief in our ability to successfully do something. We might have high confidence in some areas and not in others. For example, we might feel confident in our role at work, but not feel confident in our role as a parent.

People also assume that self-esteem and self-confidence go hand in hand, that is not the case. A person can appear and act very confident but also suffer from low self-esteem. They can act and feel confident within an area that they are competent in and still feel worthless when they compare themselves with others.

> *If we work in the same industry long enough, chances are we will become competent in that particular area. We may demonstrate and feel confident because we rarely make mistakes, have the necessary experience and knowledge, and we are able to provide relevant advice to others. However, we may notice our low self-worth when we are offered a promotion and do not believe we have the capacity to do this successfully even though others believe we can.*
>
> *We may be successful in our job and still feel a need to prove our worthiness of our salary.*

Even if we develop self-confidence in a number of areas in our life, we can still feel inferior when we compare ourselves to others in general.

> *We can feel confident in our ability to study a course, sing karaoke in front of an audience, in cooking gourmet meals, in driving a semi-trailer, but feel inadequate and unworthy when we meet someone who we perceive to be superior because they are more financially better off than us, or have a higher education or particular status.*

If we do not feel overall self-worth, no matter how many things we feel competent in doing, we will still fear failure, and fear rejection and criticism from others that we perceive to be worthier than us. For instance, we might be successful in our role at work and recognise particular talents, but feel inferior to our supervisor or our customers if we perceive them to be superior to us even though we cannot pin point exactly what it is that we believe they are superior then us in.

In saying that, a person can also have a healthy self-esteem, and not be self-confident in a particular area. For example, they may feel on an equal plane with others and not feel confident socially, or confident in a specific skill, or topic. This type of combination does not usually cause a problem, as having a healthy self-esteem will not stand in the way of developing that skill, or in obtaining knowledge or experience in a particular area when needed.

Having a healthy self-esteem means that we believe we have the capability of learning and with appropriate training, we can acquire the level of knowledge or experience of a particular new task eg., data entry, or develop a new skill eg., welding, book-keeping.

Hence, high self-esteem enables us to develop personally and professionally. On the other hand, having a belief that we do not have the capability to learn will prevent us from even trying and force us to stay in areas we have already trialled and tested.

Social confidence can also be misinterpreted as having self-confidence and self-esteem. Not all people who are socially confident have a high degree of self-worth. People with an extrovert personality who are comfortable in any social situation, able to make friends easily, often the spotlight at a party, and who have a large circle of friends, can often be misinterpreted as having a high degree of self-confidence and high self-esteem. How many times have you met someone who meets that description and noticed that they are not confident in doing certain things or going to certain places on her own? They may have the 'gift of the gab' to get themselves through that door, but their lack of self-confidence or self-worth may inevitably cause them to demonstrate otherwise in their performance.

You may have come across someone who appeared promising on their resume and presented socially confident at the interview that not long into the job did not demonstrate the skills they managed to sell during the interview.

The student who is socially confident outside the classroom and demonstrates a lack of self-esteem academically.

Some extroverts may hide their lack of self-esteem through social confidence. Their social confidence enables them to attract attention but their fear of being rejected or judged prevents others from getting too close to them. Hence, you will notice that they might have a lot of acquaintances, but very few close friendships, as they will not trust people enough to disclose or share information about themselves to achieve this. They may appear 'confident' but they may not feel 'worthy' of being accepted unconditionally.

So, **Confidence** is a state of being certain that a prediction is correct or that a decision or action is the best or most effective. **Self-confidence** is having confidence in our abilities to successfully perform certain tasks. And **Self-esteem/Self-worth** is our overall appraisal of our own worth in comparison to others. Self-worth is unconditional as it is not earned or increased by external factors, while Self-confidence which is a part of Self-worth is conditional, as it depends on our success in external factors (academic, social, financial, athletic, intellectual, strength of mind, etc.). Self-worth becomes a problem when it is measured in terms of how successful we are, or by what others think of us – that is, conditional self-worth.

CONDITIONAL VERSUS UNCONDITIONAL SELF-WORTH

People who have a healthy amount of self-worth have an unconditional self-worth. Their self-worth is not defined by anything external to their core self. This means that no matter how poor, unsuccessful, weak, sick, unattractive, immoral, or wrong a person is, or what group they belong to, or what values, beliefs or weaknesses they have, their health and happiness is still valued by others. Research has found a strong correlation between unconditional self-worth, and mental health and happiness. Alternatively, conditional self-worth controls our emotions because any threat to the conditional, the means that we use to measure our self-worth is a threat to our worthiness.

If we use our career to feed our self-worth, then we will feel worthless as soon as we lose that career.

If we feel worthy by the assets we possess, then we will feel worthless as soon as we lose those assets.

Our perception of ourselves must be accurate and measured unconditionally for it to be at a constant healthy level regardless of what is happening in our life. When our self-worth is conditional, it may increase when positive things in our life occur, but also decrease when negative things occur. We will feel worthy when things in our life are good, and unworthy when things in our life are bad.

When we enter a new relationship (positive) – we will feel worthy....as soon as that relationship ends (negative) – we will feel unworthy.

When we get a job (positive) – we will feel valued and worthy but if we lose that job (negative) – we will feel unworthy.

This occurs because the only way we have learned to feel valued, accepted, respected and worthy is through our accomplishments, and when we fail, we feel unworthy, and also expect others to see us that way. When our self-worth is unconditional, even when we fail, we do not feel unworthy because we accept that it is the outcome that has failed and that although we may have contributed to that failure, we ourselves are not a failure as a result. When we see failure as an opportunity to learn from and not something that determines our self-worth, we are more likely to grow personally. Recognising and accepting our limitations through our failures, can only lead to understanding ourselves better. And by accepting ourselves unconditionally that is, valuing the person we are regardless of our faults or weaknesses, we are more likely to tailor our life around our own needs and values rather than that of others.

Although, it is necessary to accomplish some objectives or goals in life, they should only be met to fulfil our needs and values, and not used to base our self-worth on. We need to separate our self-worth from our achievements and the judgements from others. If we don't, then our life journey will be an emotional roller-coaster ride. As such, we may respond to this by **underachieving** (low expectations and low motivation) or **over achieving** (high expectations and intense motivation to overcome the perceived weakness or failure), or both.

UNDER-ACHIEVING AND OVER-ACHIEVING

When we believe that achieving something is the key to happiness and self-worth, we will set out to fulfil this by either creating a life of low expectations that requires low motivation (such as; not trying to be a success, hanging out with people that we perceive to be 'inferior', setting easy achievable goals such as, a low paying and low responsible jobs, or the lowest level of education) that enables us to feel as though we are achieving and therefore, worthy; or by creating a life dependent on the continuous setting of unrealistic goals and high expectations that only results in increased self-criticism when they are not achieved - this only results in the cycle of setting even more unrealistic goals.

For example, we might work harder to buy that bigger and better house, or car, or get that higher income, to the one we previously thought symbolised success, in order to prove to ourselves and others that we are worthy, only to inevitably discover that with increased success, comes increased risk, increased distress and short-lived happiness.

Because we all strive for a feeling of worthiness, it makes sense that most of us would be especially motivated to succeed at, and to avoid failure of the means on which our self-worth is established on. Therefore, to successfully accept ourselves unconditionally we would need to actually embrace failure or criticism as a learning opportunity, rather than avoid it. However, if instead, when the task on which we have based our self-worth on is difficult, and we expect to fail, we are likely to become stressed, pressured, lose motivation, and therefore avoid that task. Alternatively, the positive emotional affect we get by successfully completing that task, may become addictive to a point where we may require even greater successes to feel worthy or to achieve an emotional "high".

Either performing far better than what is expected or performing far below our potential to avoid feelings of worthlessness, will inevitably result in an unfulfilling and unhappy life.

Essentially, to love ourselves unconditionally we need to love ourselves no matter who we are, what we have, what we have done, or what others think of us. We need to stop impressing others and worrying about what they think of us.

> *Accepting ourselves unconditionally means taking good care of ourselves and meeting our needs and values. It means making our own health and happiness a top priority.*

So how do we become conditioned to meeting everyone else's needs and not ours?

How do we get to a point where we allow our lives to be controlled by the need to please others, and the need to be accepted by others even at the expense of our own needs and happiness? - How does our life become so conditional?

Although feasible, without fully understanding how, it will not be easy to address our self-worth properly. The aim of this book is to address self-worth and to develop the necessary skills to maintain it and this will be covered in Part Two of this book.

CONTRIBUTING FACTORS TO THE DEVELOPMENT OF CONDITIONAL SELF-WORTH

So how do we develop conditional self-worth?

We are all driven by positive self-regard, that is, the quality of being worthy of esteem and of respect. We achieve this by the positive regard we experience from others throughout our life. Without this self-regard, we will feel worthless and not become all that we can be.

Although we are born with a 'clean slate', the complex cognitive system that is necessary to assess beliefs about ourselves develops overtime as we grow up. As children we assess our environment as simply being friendly or hostile and, satisfying or frustrating, and we quickly learn that we typically evoke either acceptance or rejection from others. We also interpret these early social experiences into pride or shame. The influences we receive from society contribute significantly to the development of our self-esteem. The foundation of our self-esteem then significantly influence the way we see ourselves and the world as adults. From day one, we have been conditioned to base our worth on our accomplishments? As a child we were taught that:-

Getting an 'A' meant we were smart and therefore worthy. We may have received praise or a reward when we got that 'A' and only received, "You can do better" or "Why didn't you get an 'A'?" when we got an 'A-' or 'B+'.

Being in the 'lead role' in the play meant we were important and popular. We may have received a pat on the back and "Well done!", but when we didn't get the lead role we got "Why are you in a minor role this term?", "Why did the teacher think Amy was better then you?".

We may have throughout our childhood heard our parents only talk about us to others only whenever we accomplished something.

We quickly learned that 'being perfect or the best and nothing less' resulted in being accepted or valued by others.

We are also compared to our peers from an early age:-

"What did Billy get for his assignment?"

"Why was Sally selected for the team and not you?"

"See how Sally is able to talk confidently in front of the class you should be able to do that too"

"Why can't you be more like Sally?"

We learned from this that being unique or different or average at something is not valued by others.

When we are given positive attention only when we achieve, and shunned, ignored or criticised when we don't, the message we receive from society is that 'winners' are acknowledged and 'losers' are not, and that it is what we do, that makes us worthy, not who we are. When we are constantly compared to others, the message we receive is that we have to be the best at everything we do, and that second best or being good at some things and not others is not an option, if we are to be valued and accepted by others.

As we grow up, our parents, teachers, peers, the media, and other significant influences also continuously send us the message throughout our life, that we only deserve what we need when we show that we are worthy, rather than just because we need it. This is **conditional positive self-regard**:

As a child at school, we learn about 'Conditional Worth' early in the piece when we were told, "If you give me your lunch, you can play with me today". Or"If you finish your school work, you can have a drink".

As a child we get a dessert only if we finish our dinner; we get a sweet when we behave at the shops; we get a hug and a kiss when our babysitter says we've been good; we get a book read to us before bed when we've been good.

As a teenager, we are able to have a party when we get a good report card; we get rewarded and praised when we top our class.

As an adult, we are accepted when we have the car, the house, the job, the status.

We all need and therefore seek positive regard from others. Growing up shaping our life around a society that may or may not have our best interest at heart can only result in an unhealthy and unhappy life. Ultimately, this 'conditioning' leads us to develop **conditional positive self-regard** whereby we accept ourselves only if we meet the standards and expectations set by others – even if these standards are unrealistic, or do not meet our own needs, values or personality. When we find ourselves not able to meet these standards, we are also unable to maintain any sense of self-worth.

So how do we develop *unconditional self-worth*?

The answer is – living a life without conditions of worth and accepting ourselves unconditionally – the **real self**, rather than living a life with conditions of worth and only accepting ourselves conditionally – the **ideal self**. It is not too late or impossible to recondition the way we perceive ourselves and the world, and the way we measure our self-worth.

INCONGRUITY BETWEEN THE REAL SELF AND THE IDEAL SELF

If throughout our life we seek and receive unconditional positive regard and self-regard, then we have a high chance of developing a **'real self'**. However, if we allow ourselves to live with conditions of worth and receive only conditional positive regard and self-regard, we will instead develop an **'ideal self'**. The ideal self is not real, it is the person we believe society want us to be, the standards we believe we must meet but can't - the "I should". On the other hand, the real self is the true person that we are, our own unconditional self - the "I am".

Our real self is the person we know ourselves to be – our strengths and weaknesses, our true beliefs, passions, needs, interests, opinions and attitudes, our unique traits, likes and dislikes, our mannerism, our personal values and personal goals, dreams and aspirations. Our real self is who we really are and what we are meant to adapt our life to. When we live our life according to what we think will provide us with positive regard from others, we live a lie. We may adapt our life to consist of the things we believe others accept us for, even if we know deep down that these things do not make us happy. We may attend university not because we want to, but because that is what we believe we need to do to be accepted by our parents. We may hang around people that we know don't think like us, or have the same interests as us, because we believe that they are the type of people society accept as worthy. We may dress a particular style that we believe others accept even though we know it is not us. How many times, have we made choices in our life based on what we 'should' do, rather than on what we really 'want' to do?

We are programmed from a young age to forge a life around what society portrays as 'the norm' – rather than adapting our life around the person we really are –'our true self'. When we adapt our life according to what we think society or others will accept we go against our grain – we lose ourselves. It's like trying to fit a square block into a round hole.

> *A creative person, who is conditioned to live a 'neat, tidy, and highly organised' life, is likely to struggle, if living a 'non-structured' life unleashes their creativity.*
>
> *A person who appears unmotivated and disinterested in obtaining a highly responsible job because he/she prefers to 'work to live' rather than 'live to work' may be misunderstood by others as being lazy.*

When we strive to become the person we believe we 'should' be, instead of the person we really 'want' to be, we are continuously going against our grain. This conflict between the 'real self' and the 'ideal self' only leads to a life of suffering and unhappiness, as we continuously strive to become someone that we are not, or achieve something we don't really want.

When we are forced to cope with the incongruity between our 'ideal self' and our 'real self', and feel threatened, we may employ defence mechanisms such as, Denial or Perceptual Distortion to cope.

DEFENCE MECHANISMS

When we are in **Denial** we avoid the threatening situation altogether. For example, we may never collect our test result so that we do not have to face failure and by avoiding it, we also refuse to perceive it. We may use denial when a fact is too uncomfortable to accept as true even when there is sufficient evidence supporting it or admit the fact and its seriousness but deny responsibility.

> *Alcoholics and addicts believe their own denial to avoid the agonising reality that their addiction controls their life and is destructive. They will also blame their addiction on others or on past negative situations or experiences rather than admit responsibility.*

We may also use **Perceptual Distortion** to reinterpret a situation so that it does not appear as threatening. For example, we may blame the lecturer for our poor grade on a test. *"If the lecturer was better at teaching the subject, or did not have such a thick accent, or did not put trick questions, I would have passed my test".*

Defence mechanisms may work temporarily at alleviating emotional distress triggered by negative experiences, however, the more we use a defence, the greater the distance created between the real and the ideal self. The greater the incongruity the more anxiety we experience, and more threatened we become by situations, and the more we rely on defence mechanisms. This vicious cycle prevents us from growing personally, as the key to growth is to face challenging situations, not avoid them.

Therefore, while it is clear that unconditional self-worth is the key to happiness and wellbeing, to achieve this we must first accept our 'real self' – the 'I am' and live our life according to our true needs, values and personality – the 'I want'.

Our perception of ourselves must be accurate, and what we use to measure our self-worth must also be unconditional. When we accept ourselves for who we are, and shape our life according to what we feel is right and genuine, we will develop a healthy self-worth. Conversely, when our perception of ourselves is based on the inaccurate and unproven opinions of others, or on our assumptions; and/or the contingencies of what we believe we must do or be in order to be a person of worth, and value is based on others' criterion, then we are wasting our life trying to be someone we are not and don't really want to be. Therefore, accepting our 'real' self and living the life we are meant to, can only result in a complete and fulfilling life.

With self-worth comes the confidence to live life to the full. It enables you to be happy and to lead a better life.

When you have a healthy Self-Esteem:

- You will recognise and celebrate your successes and achievements.
- You will value and utilise your strengths.
- You may have doubts and don't know all the answers.
- You don't put yourself down.

- If you make a mistake you're happy to forgive yourself.
- You are humble.
- You don't judge yourself too harshly.
- You don't beat yourself up for your weaknesses.
- You are happy setting yourself targets and goals, and value any feedback.
- You have developed a good balance between different parts of your life.

So, what changes to our life can we expect once we have self-worth?

Self-esteem has wider consequences on our life than self-confidence. It affects our relationships with other people, what kind of events and people that we attract into our life, our mental and physical health, and more. In fact, self-esteem plays a significant role in our life. If there is anything you want to change in your life - whether it is a specific problem or if you want to improve in some area - you can only do so by improving your self-esteem.

HOW LOW SELF-ESTEEM CAN AFFECT YOUR LIFE

There are numerous factors that can affect the development of a healthy self-esteem; the most common ones are, a dysfunctional childhood, unhealthy relationships, and unrealistic standards and expectations of oneself and/or from others. When your self-esteem is 'stunted', dealing with day to day life stressors (an inevitable part of life), and developing genuine and healthy relationships become extremely challenging. Other aspects of your life such as, hobbies, social and vocational activities also become limited and even non-existent. Fear of failure and fear of rejection become influential factors in your every action and decision making to a point that it can restrict your life immensely.

When you fear rejection and rely on unhealthy coping mechanisms like avoidance and/or over-pleasing, it will have a negative effect on your relationships. Over-pleasing the people in your life in the most part is likely to result in a 'win-lose' relationship, with you losing out and the other person gaining the most from the relationship. When you are doing all the hard work to maintain this relationship only to receive very little in return, it won't take you long to start feeling unvalued and resentful towards that person. A relationship that is mostly based on you making the other person feel valued and secure, is a toxic relationship that will damage your self-esteem further.

Many clients have said to me that they prefer to have someone in their life even if they are toxic than to be alone. When your self-esteem is low, you believe that you are not good enough to be accepted by others that you perceive to be better than you. Therefore, you are likely to accept people in your life that should not even be there. The kind of people that manipulate you, and have control over you, take advantage of you, put you down, and abuse you – toxic people. The belief that you have to be liked by everyone you meet is not always feasible. Some people may have issues that can stand in the way of developing a healthy relationship with you, others may have personality traits that you may not 'click' with – not being able to develop a genuine, healthy relationship with someone may not even be your doing.

Not only can low self-esteem affect your relationships, but it can also interfere in your social life. The fear of being rejected by others or as some of my clients put it, 'being found out that you are a fraud', can interfere with you opening up and interacting comfortably in social situations. Negative thoughts and concerns about being judged and/or rejected by the other person can cause you so much anxiety that you are likely to continuously avoid social situations, and therefore miss out on developing a sense of belonging – a very important factor in feeling valued.

Fear of failure can also be another indication of low self-esteem that can restrict you in life. Fear of failure can often be a barrier to bringing into your life, the things that can give you a sense of achievement, stimulation and purpose. Undertaking hobbies, volunteering, work, training and studies, can be very daunting for someone who expects to fail and not only feel like a failure but also be seen by others as a failure. Taking a step out of their comfort is liable to cause them so much anxiety, that staying within their comfort zone and missing out on 'life', can be for some an easier way of life. Unfortunately, living a life too within your comfort zone where you do not get the chance to acquire whatever it is you aspire to in life, or not taking on opportunities that you are presented with to prove your abilities, and/or to further develop your skills, can often result in the development of depression and an unfulfilling life.

People who suffer from low self-esteem will go to great lengths to hide their weaknesses. We all have qualities, and we all have weaknesses, but we all don't have the same qualities and weaknesses. A weakness in someone else might be a quality within you. You might be uncoordinated while someone is, but you might be creative while that same person is not. Determining what your qualities and weaknesses are, is part of developing your own identity that cannot happen without trial and error. How can you know if you are creative if you don't try something that will test this out? And what if you fail at that activity and find out that you are not creative. Then you just accept it as one of your weaknesses. People with a healthy self-esteem tend to accept their weaknesses and are comfortable sharing this information with others.

They know their strengths and their weaknesses, and avoid opportunities that rely on strengths they do not have, and instead pursue those that focus on their strengths. Why accept an employment opportunity that relies heavily on creative abilities that you do not possess, when you might perform better in another position that relies on one or more of your qualities? While failure is something that everyone encounters throughout their life, and it's a vital component in determining your identity, acknowledging your weaknesses and qualities unfortunately, isn't an easy thing to do when you have low self-esteem. When you actually believe that you mostly have weaknesses and have very few qualities, accepting that promotion at work for instance, might not be an easy thing to do, especially when you expect to fail, and fear that failure. What can only result from this situation, is a lot of anxiety, and to avoid anxiety, you are more than likely to avoid that opportunity. For this reason and more, it is important to have a strong sense of worth.

Diagram 4.1 below demonstrates some of the important aspects for a fulfilling and well-balanced life that can provide you with a sense of purpose, sense of stimulation, and a sense of belonging. If you can work towards attaining most of these, then you are more likely to be happier and healthier both mentally and physically. The key to attaining these easily however, is to first work towards developing a healthy self-esteem, without this it can be an uphill battle.

Diagram 4.1

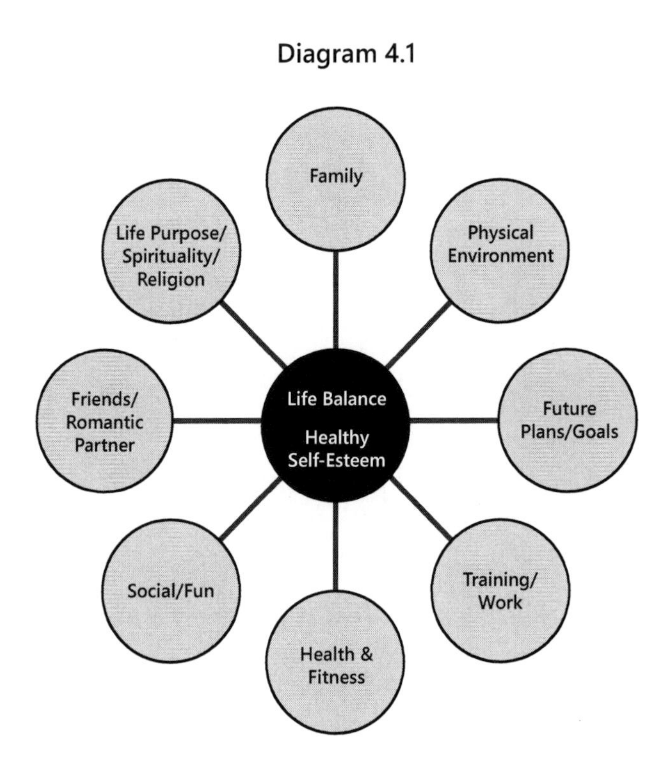

SO HOW DO YOU DEVELOP A HEALTHY SELF-ESTEEM?

As previously mentioned, the experiences and relationships we have throughout our life, negative and positive, and how we deal with them, and the interpretation we make, play a major role in the development and maintenance of our self-esteem. We may not always have control over the situation we are in, but we do have control over what we interpret of that situation, and even whether or not we stay in that situation. For example, if you are in a toxic relationship you can't control the other person's behaviour, but you can control your perception of that situation. Forming an accurate interpretation of the situation, so that you develop a clear understanding of what is actually happening at the time, is a necessary step in preventing unjustified personalisation and self-blame, and damage to your self-esteem.

How we interpret what is going on both internally and externally is crucial in forming a healthy perception of ourselves. In order to achieve this, we need to assess our surroundings and our thoughts in an objective manner. Low self-esteem sufferers commonly form subjective interpretations. They do not take into consideration other external contributing factors outside of what they are thinking or feeling. So, if they are criticised about something they immediately accept it without first analysing whether that criticism is justified or not. Similarly, if they fail at something, they immediately accept blame without first ascertaining the contributing factors. This bad habit of thinking such as, personalisation and self-blame, is commonly developed in early childhood, when skills in rationalisation may not have been fully developed to form an accurate interpretation of a situation. Unfortunately, once this habit sets in, the worse it becomes as we continue the spiral of misinterpreting throughout our lives. This pattern of thinking becomes so second nature to us that the negative thinking cycle can become too difficult to break – hence why 'just thinking positive to feel positive' is a lot easier said than done.

To break the cycle of negative thinking, you have to objectively analyse, (a) all external information presented to you in everyday life, both negative and positive such as, outcomes (both negative or positive), criticism and actions from others, and (b) all internal information such as, self-criticism and negative thoughts. Diagram 4.2 illustrates the correct process of analysing situations to form an accurate interpretation.

For example, if you are given a criticism by someone, the first and utmost step you must take is to 'objectively screen' that criticism before even accepting it as true. By screening it, you are collecting as much objective evidence as you can, as proof for and against that criticism, before you deem it true or false.

Being objective means that you rely only on evidence outside of what you think or what you feel. That's the difficult part of this process, but once you master it, you are on your way to building a healthy sense of self-worth. What makes this process difficult, is changing the long-term bad habit of analysing information subjectively that is, assessing information based on what you think is going on rather than what is actually going on. Breaking a bad habit is not easy in any case. However, once you learn the technique of assessing information objectively, you will be able to determine whether a criticism is 'constructive' or 'destructive', and respond to that criticism in a proactive manner, rather than personalising it, and responding to it in a manner that will certainly lead to further damage to your self-worth.

Destructive criticism, that is, criticism that is not backed up by sufficient evidence, is aimed at manipulating and/or putting you down. Destructive criticism is a practice commonly used by people who also suffer from low self-esteem. These people will put you down either because they are intimidated by something they believe you have over them such as, certain skills or traits or qualities that they do not see in themselves, and they will target you because they know you will just take it – which further empowers them. In some cases, however, the criticism may not necessarily be deliberately aimed at putting you down, or to manipulate you, but instead a misunderstanding based on insufficient evidence. In these instances, the person is likely to accept their mistake and right their opinion accordingly. These types of people are likely to have healthy self-esteem and be assertive and confident.

Differentiating between toxic and healthy relationships is a must when developing and protecting your self-esteem. After all, having a sense of belonging, and feeling valued by others, is one of the major contributing factors in the development and maintenance of a healthy self-esteem. And while an important step in developing a healthy self-esteem is to distinguish between a toxic and nontoxic relationship, asserting yourself to try and resolve a situation may not be an easy thing to do without a strong self-esteem. Without assertiveness skills you are likely to have poor self-esteem, and as discussed earlier, without a healthy self-esteem you will find it too difficult to assert yourself in these situations. Assertiveness skills is an important skill that will be covered later on in this book.

Assessing situations in an objective manner is not only useful in helping you develop healthy relationships and self-esteem, but also in understanding yourself better and in forming an identity. Determining, and most importantly 'accepting' your weaknesses, and your strengths, is a necessary step in developing your own identity, and that is where the objective 'screening' process can be beneficial. People spend too much energy worrying about having weaknesses, and others seeing these weaknesses. There is not one person on this planet that does not have weaknesses. From day one we are conditioned by external influences such as, parents, friends, teachers, media, and others that having weaknesses is not a normal thing to have. There is too much focus on trying to be 'perfect' and in getting lost in the process of trying. This conditioning starts in early childhood. For example, as a child we are expected and conditioned to believe that it is 'normal' to obtain straight 'A's in all subjects in school. If that was a realistic expectation, wouldn't the majority of students be achieving this? The first most important thing you must do if you want to live a happy and healthy life is to accept that having weaknesses is normal. And that we all don't have the same strengths and weaknesses. One of your weaknesses may be a strength in another person, just like a weakness in them may be a strength in you. You might be creative, but not organised while someone else might be organised but not creative. Imagine if everyone in the world had the same strengths and weakness, how could that work? Therefore, an important step in developing an identity is to first determine and accept your weaknesses and strengths, and adapt your life accordingly. Only then can you become fully content and live a healthy life. Putting energy on the areas in your life that focuses on your strengths will be a lot easier than wasting precious energy and time doing something that does not come easy to you, and that is going against your grain.

Diagram 4.2 demonstrates how 'Objective Screening' can be effective in identifying true weaknesses. If there is sufficient evidence that indicates that a constructive criticism is accurate, then you must accept it as a weakness. While it is possible to change some weaknesses, for example, poor time management, the effort you will put into changing it will depend on how much of a negative impact that weakness is having on your life. If that weakness does not have much of an impact on your life to warrant putting the effort into changing it, then you just simply accept it and work your life around it, but most importantly – accept it. Once you accept your weaknesses, only then will you be able to cope with someone else pointing it out to you.

Once you know yourself well and accept your true self, instead of trying to 'fit into a life that is not you', you will find that it will be a lot easier to create a 'life that actually fits you'. In order to achieve this, you need to master the art of screening what is happening around you in an objective way. Learning to screen objectively may not be an easy task to master initially, especially when you are having to objectively screen something so subjective. Trying to push aside your emotions to assess a criticism or a self-putdown objectively, will not be an easy task to do first hand and may require practice – and practice makes perfect. Chapter Five explains the practical application of Objective (Evidence-Based) Screening and provides examples.

Part Two, Chapter Five, is the practical part of the book that will teach you the techniques to develop a healthy and strong self-esteem.

Diagram 4.2

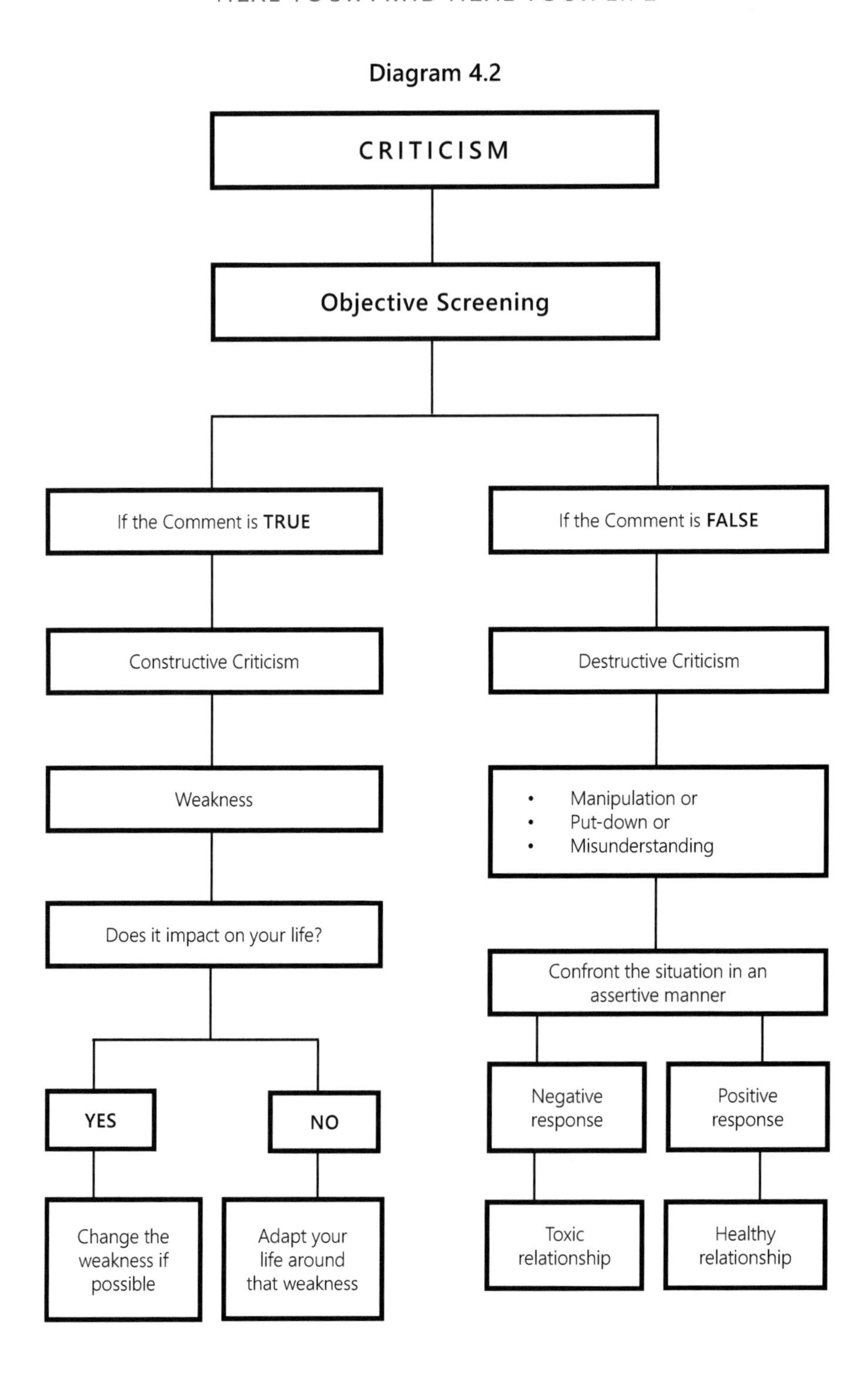
CRITICISM
Objective Screening
If the Comment is TRUE
If the Comment is FALSE
Constructive Criticism
Destructive Criticism
Weakness
• Manipulation or
• Put-down or
• Misunderstanding
Does it impact on your life?
Confront the situation in an assertive manner
YES
NO
Negative response
Positive response
Change the weakness if possible
Adapt your life around that weakness
Toxic relationship
Healthy relationship

PART TWO

PRACTICAL

CHAPTER FIVE

THE OBJECTIVE SCREENING TECHNIQUE

"The happiness of your life depends on the quality of your thoughts" – Curiano.com

COGNITIVE Behavioural Therapy (CBT), originally designed to treat depression, is effective for a variety of conditions, including mood, anxiety, personality, eating, addiction, dependence, and psychotic disorders. Mainstream cognitive behavioral therapy assumes that changing irrational thinking leads to change in affect and behavior..The goal of Cognitive Behavioral Therapy is not to diagnose a person with a particular disease, but to look at them as a whole and decide what needs to be fixed and typically it is their thinking pattern.

I am a strong supporter of Beck's Cognitive Behavioural Therapy and have found this to be an extremely useful treatment technique particularly, for clients who suffer from Anxiety and/or Depression. However, in saying that, CBT can be a complicated technique to understand enough to apply it well. The Objective Screening Technique is a simplified method that works along the same concept as that of CBT.

The Objective Screening (Evidence-Based) Technique is a useful technique in analysing criticism from others, and negative self-talk, objectively and accurately. It is a method of assessing oneself that is based on evidence rather than on assumptions only. People who have a healthy self-esteem, derive conclusions about themselves based on objective evidence only, not subjective. The conclusions they draw are never based on their own beliefs, thoughts or feelings but instead only on factual and tangible information.

When you rely solely on your own thoughts, beliefs, and emotions to make a judgement on a subjective matter, and these are mostly negative, you can get yourself into a spiral of mental self-abuse and negativity. In saying that, I am not discounting relying on intuition or body language. Some people are very good at picking up minor details, reading body language, and have strong intuition. However, to ensure that you are making an accurate conclusion about something that you may have picked up intuitively or through body language, a wise step would be to confirm this by also collecting objective evidence. Body language and/or intuition can be a useful prompt, but relying on evidence-based information is a must for mental well-being. For example, you might pick up through body language that your work-colleague is annoyed, but how do you know that it is you that they are annoyed with unless you ask them?

Objective Screening may be a simple concept and may appear to be a simple technique to apply however, collecting the evidence objectively may initially take some practice to master as it is not an easy task to find objective evidence for something so subjective. However, this technique should eventually become an automatic thought process and new habit of thinking. Practicing this new technique on criticism that you have received in the past and that you have been hanging on to is a good place to start, and a good way of getting a 'clean slate'. The more you analyse these criticisms and let go of the ones that do not have any evidence to support them, the cleaner your slate will become. Letting go of unjustified criticisms that you have received from others and self-criticism, and only accepting those that are supported by evidence is the first step in your journey to recovery. Attaining a 'clean slate' while continuing to apply the Objective Screening Technique to current situations will not only result in you finding out what you're true weaknesses are, but also help you filter current and incoming information before you accept them. Diagram 5.1 demonstrates this process.

DIAGRAM 5.1

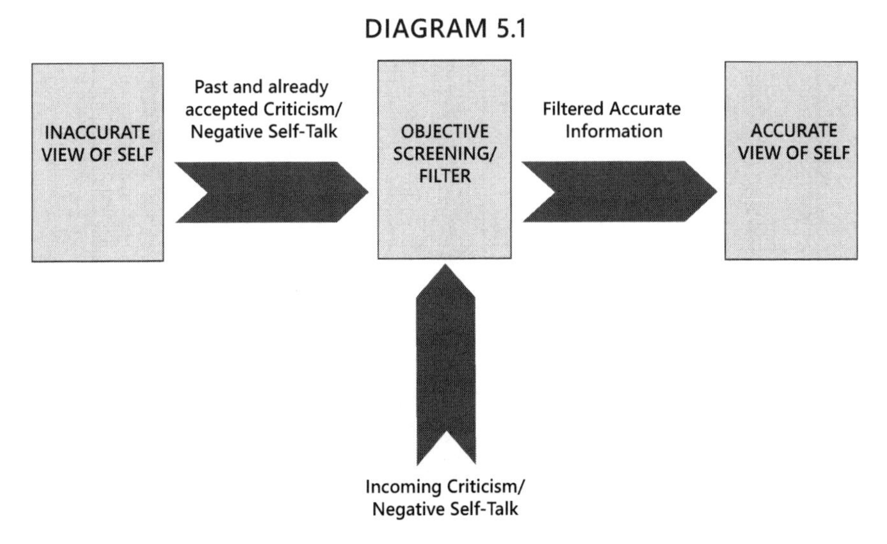

OBJECTIVE (EVIDENCE-BASED) SCREENING

To assess something objectively, it needs to be neutral, bias free, and relating to, or based on verifiable evidence or facts instead of on attitude, belief, feeling, or opinion. It is the opposite of subjective. Mastering the Objective Screening (CBT based) Technique may initially take some practice. It is not an easy task to push aside your emotions to assess something objectively as you are required to think in order to perform this task. Emotions can interfere in the process of thinking especially negative emotions that can manifest in physiological symptoms. Once the technique becomes a new habit of thinking, and your emotions are more regulated and less intense, it will become a lot easier to perform. It is a technique that should be utilised on an ongoing basis throughout the rest of your life.

Objective Screening involves collecting tangible evidence external to your own beliefs, thoughts and feelings, much like you would do when forming an opinion on something – you would first collect your facts and then draw a conclusion based on those facts. If someone stated their opinion on a particular topic, unless you had evidence that proved them right, you wouldn't just accept their opinion as true, so why would you just accept a negative self-criticism or a criticism from someone without first seeking evidence to either confirm or discard it. This is the concept behind Objective Screening.

The evidence collected must be detached from what you think and feel about the subject matter. In the same way that the legal system base's its verdict solely on facts, so should we with the information we receive externally and that enter our minds.

OBJECTIVE SCREENING STEPS

When looking for evidence for and against a criticism or a negative thought that was made either in the past or present, you need to take into account all comments (both negative and positive) that you can recall, that were made by people throughout your life. People who have had an opportunity to have evaluated you on that criticism. For example, if your current employer criticised you of being "disorganised", before accepting it as a constructive criticism, you would be wise to firstly screen this criticism objectively by seeking a) comments made by others who have had the opportunity to know you well enough to be able to make that judgement of you on that particular skill. For example, teachers, parents, siblings, partners and even ex-partners, friends, current and past work colleagues, current and past employers, customers and extended family et cetera. You could also look at situations where this skill has been demonstrated not only in recent situations but throughout your life. For example, meeting deadlines such as, work responsibilities and school assignments, organising the kids or staff, or perhaps having completed a personality test at some stage in your life whereby this skill was assessed.

A vital point to remember while collecting this evidence is to NEVER take your own beliefs and feelings into account if you want to remain objective. In other words, you do not include "I feel disorganised, therefore I am disorganised" or "I believe I am disorganised". The evidence you would accept include; a) criticisms that were made, b) compliments that were made, c) not having received criticism when that skill was demonstrated, and d) other means in which the skill was demonstrated. The evidence collected should be taken from all phases in your life including, childhood, adolescence and adulthood, and include everyone that you can recall who during that period would have had an opportunity to be impacted by that particular skills either in a positive or negative way. For example, the teachers, principle, parents, siblings, students, coaches et cetera who would have spent a period of time with you to either have been impacted by that skill or lack of skill, or have either criticised or complimented, or have not criticised you on that skill. The evidence collected should also include every opportunity that you had throughout your life where that skill was demonstrated. For example, assignments, attending meetings on time, organising a group assignment, juggling a number of activities, paying bills on time, organising your work responsibilities et cetera.

Once all the objective evidence has been collected, your conclusion on whether that self-criticism or criticism from others is accurate will be based on the side that shows the majority of evidence, even if there is some evidence showing on the other side.

The fact that most people that you have encountered in your life do not agree with that criticism, and the fact that there is more demonstrable evidence, should indicate that the criticism is not true and therefore that destructive criticism should be rejected. On the other-hand, if there was sufficient support for that criticism based on the majority of people agreeing with the criticism and insufficient evidence demonstrating that you possess that skill, then you must accept the constructive criticism.

The Objective Screening Technique is an activity that should be applied throughout the rest of your life to accurately analyse oncoming criticism from others and your own self-criticism. The following Chapter covers the correct way to assess negative outcomes such as, failure using the Objective Screening Technique.

While Diagrams 5.2, 5.3 and 5.4 on the following pages provide examples of how to perform the Objective Screening on negative self-talk, this technique can also be applied to objectively screen criticism from others. The diagram can be used to practice the technique, but after you have mastered it you will find that you will automatically perform it mentally. The Activity on Page 80 is designed to practice the technique and it is highly recommended that you do these activities on a daily basis to reinforce this new pattern of thinking.

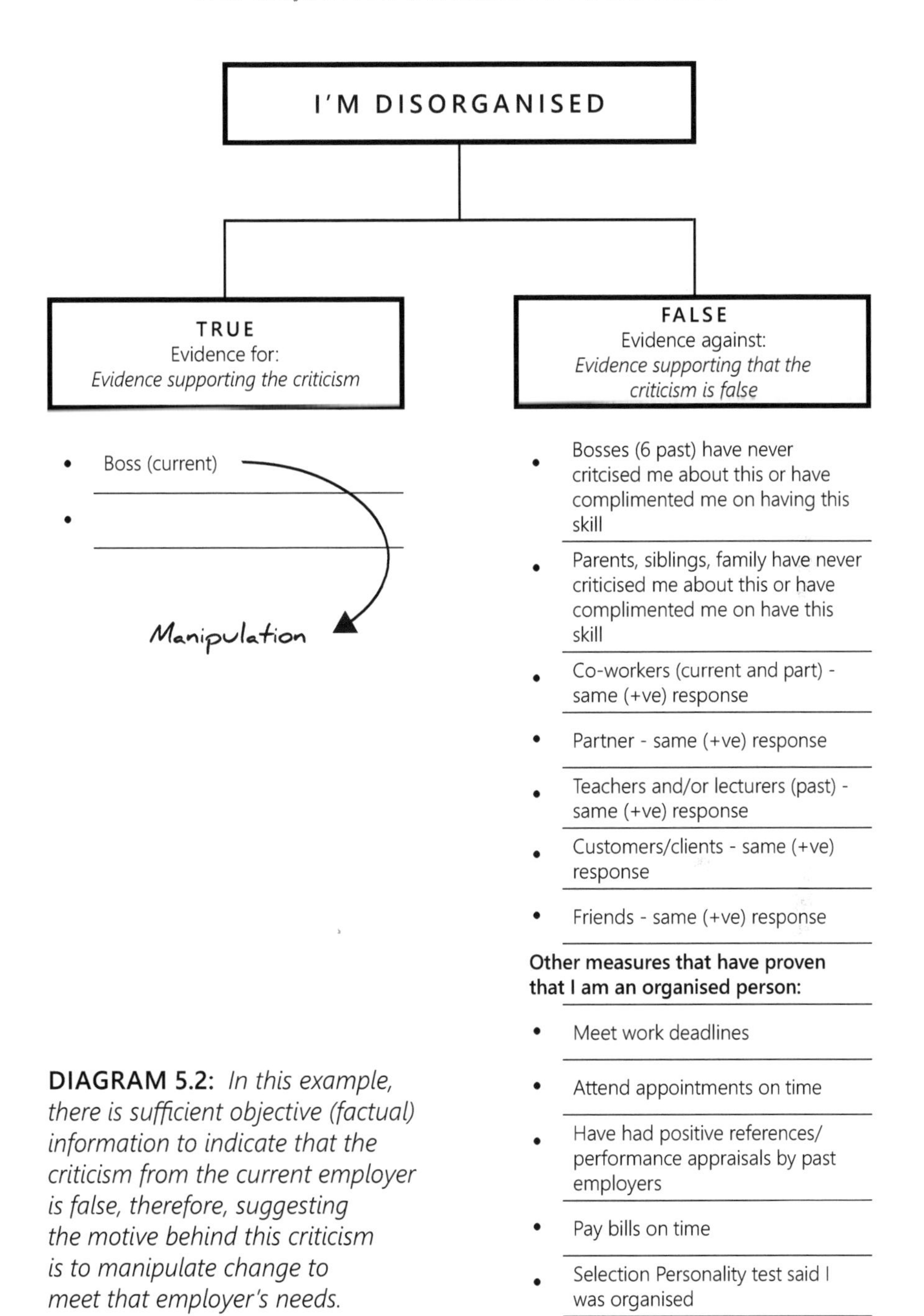

DIAGRAM 5.2: *In this example, there is sufficient objective (factual) information to indicate that the criticism from the current employer is false, therefore, suggesting the motive behind this criticism is to manipulate change to meet that employer's needs.*

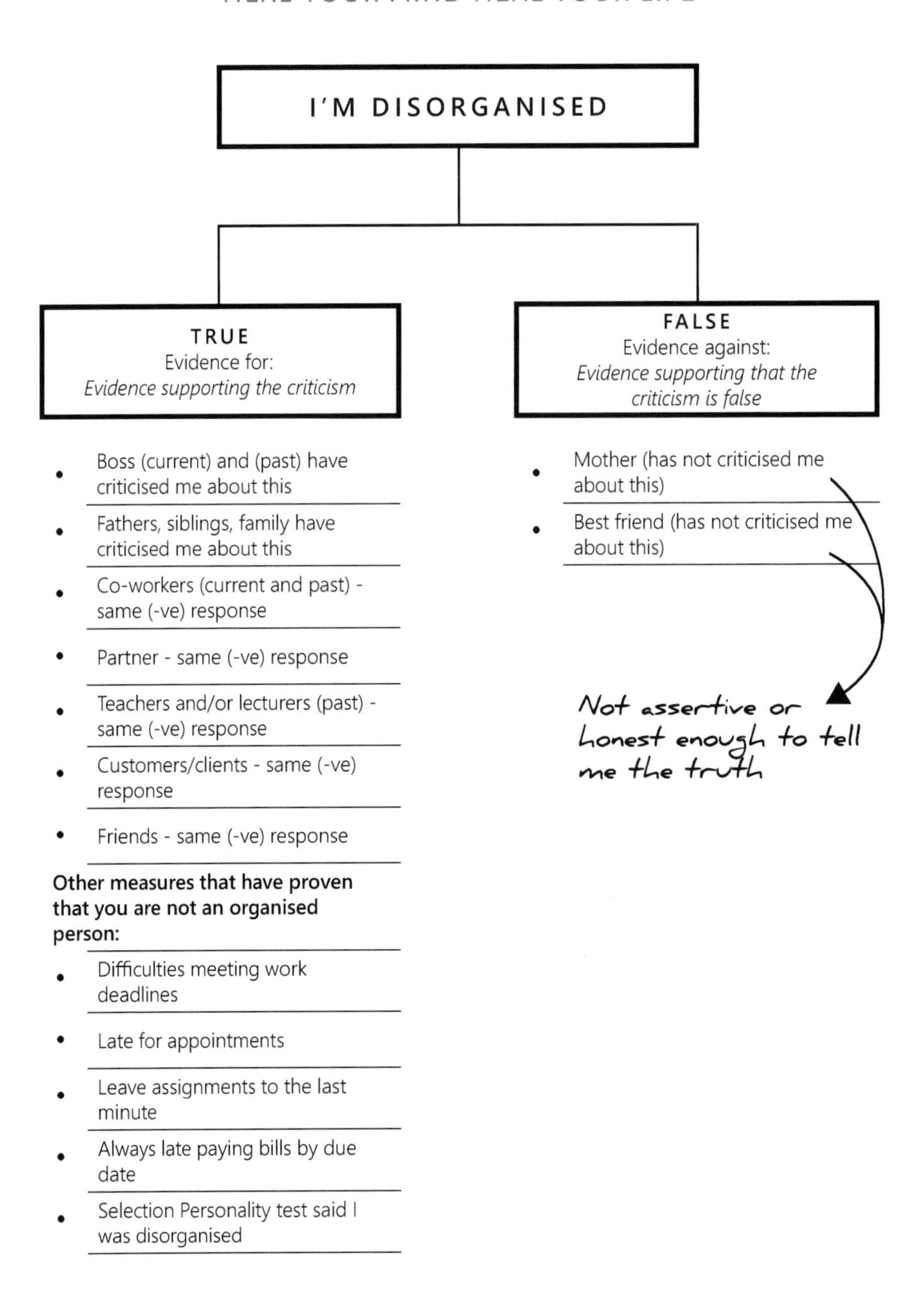

DIAGRAM 5.3: *In this example, there is sufficient objective (factual) information to indicate that the criticism from the current employer is justified and constructive criticism is being used to encourage positive change.*

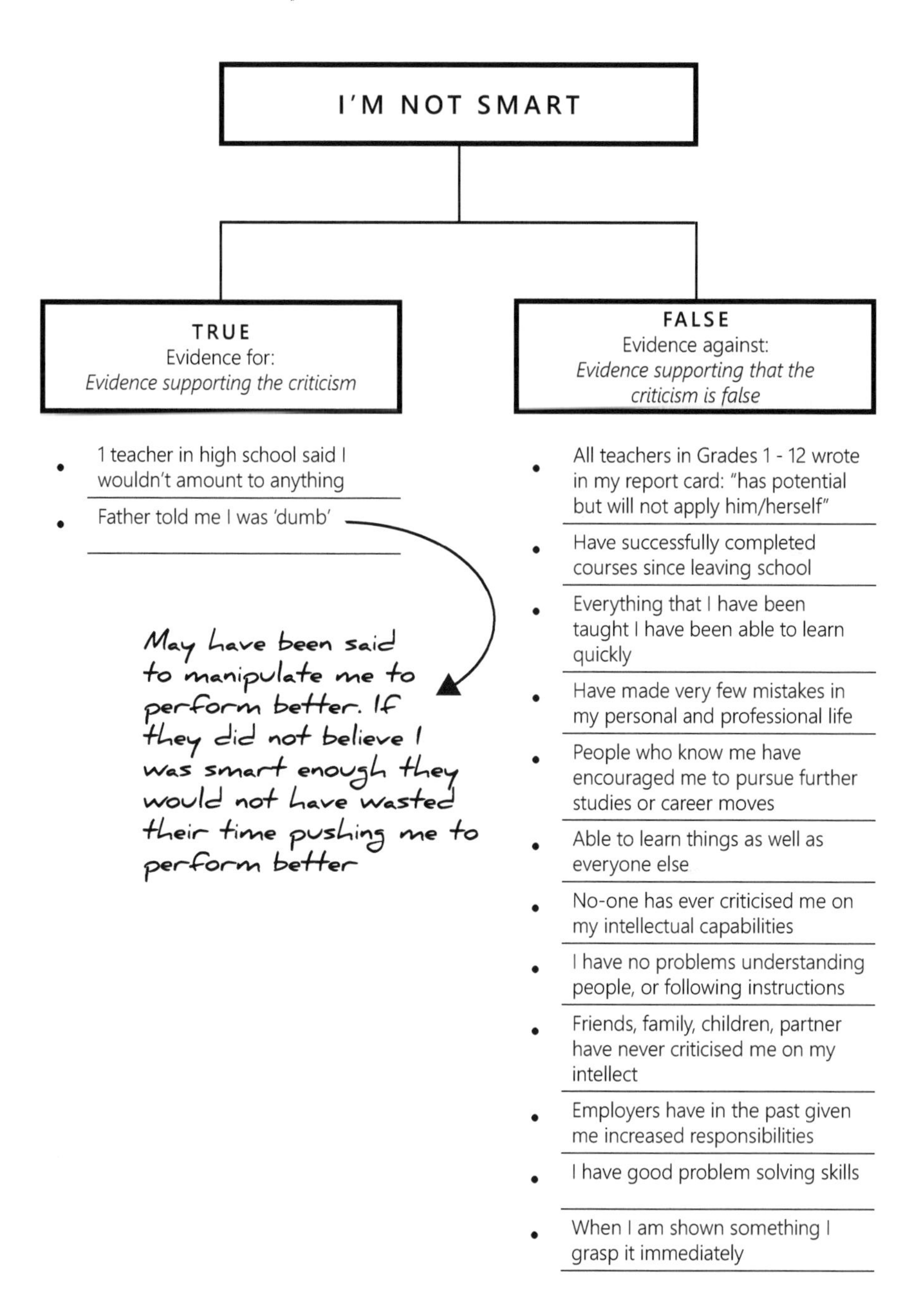

DIAGRAM 5.4: *In this example, there is insufficient objective (factual) information to indicate that the negative self-putdown is accurate and therefore should be rejected.*

HOMEWORK

ACTIVITY 5A:

Using the template on pages 81 and 82, write three self-criticisms you have had in the last week or so, and three criticisms you received from others, and the objective evidence for and against these criticisms. Note: Be mindful of not including what you believe or feel as part of your evidence.

HOMEWORK

TRUE
Evidence for:
Evidence supporting the criticism

FALSE
Evidence against:
Evidence supporting that the criticism is false

HOMEWORK

TRUE Evidence for: *Evidence supporting the criticism*	FALSE Evidence against: *Evidence supporting that the criticism is false*
• ______	• ______
• ______	• ______
• ______	• ______
• ______	• ______
• ______	• ______
• ______	• ______
• ______	• ______
• ______	• ______
• ______	• ______
• ______	• ______
• ______	• ______
• ______	• ______
• ______	• ______
• ______	• ______
• ______	• ______
• ______	• ______

CHAPTER SIX

PERFECTIONISM AND HIGH UNREALISTIC STANDARDS AND THE IMPACT ON SELF-ESTEEM

"Those who have a strong sense of love and belonging have the courage to be imperfect" – Brene Brown, Ph. D. LMSW.

PEOPLE who have perfectionistic habits of thinking are motivated to live 'the perfect life' in 'the perfect way'. They will try to achieve this even at the expense of their own health and their relationships. As a result, they can suffer burnout, depression, anxiety and/or excessive stress, and health conditions such as, Chronic Fatigue Syndrome. They set unrealistic standards and expectations of themselves and they will do everything in their power to achieve these goals and expect the same from others. Unfortunately, striving to achieve unrealistic goals and/or goals within unrealistic timeframes, is not only an exhausting way to live by, but also detrimental to their health and well-being and those of others, particularly, their partners and children.

Perfectionism is not the same as striving for excellence. People who follow excellence in a healthy way take genuine pleasure in working to meet high standards. Perfectionists on the other hand are aggravated by self-doubt and worries of disapproval, ridicule, and disagreement. Children who are brought up by parents with strong perfectionistic thinking and behaviour can often end up suffering from low self-esteem and develop a poor sense of identity, and even carry on the same perfectionistic patterns of behaviour throughout their life.

There are two typical ways that someone can develop perfectionistic thinking and behaviour. The first is through the observation of a parent or influential figure throughout their childhood and teen years. By observing a parent who has high perfectionism, they can become conditioned to believe that the person's standards and beliefs are the 'norm', and as a result will continue to live their life with this norm as their benchmark. In a lot of cases, these standards and expectations are forced upon their children. A child living under this type of parenting will quickly learn from a young age that employing similar behaviour will prevent criticism and/or punishment. In an attempt to avoid criticism and gain recognition and acceptance, they will put a lot of effort into everything they do. They will go through life holding on to the false belief that others have the same expectations of them, and therefore will continue the same unhealthy behaviour.

People who have developed perfectionism this way typically demonstrate this type of behaviour by always aspiring to be top achievers and by not allowing themselves to make even a single error. They are always on the vigilance for imperfections and weaknesses in themselves and others. They tend to be inflexible thinkers who are on the lookout for deviations from the rules or the norm.

Another common way that perfectionism can be developed is by having an unhealthy sense of self-worth and therefore, fearing criticism, punishment, and/or rejection. For example, when someone is fearful of making a mistake because they believe that it will result in criticism, consequence or rejection, they will do everything in their power to make sure that the task is completed 'perfectly'.

Perfectionism is a coping mechanism for poor self-esteem, that is typically employed by people who have passive, over-pleasing and non-confrontational temperaments. Until they address their self-esteem they will continue to live an exhausting and anxious life. They will constantly feel the need to over-analyse, over-please, and over-commit to avoid confrontation, criticism and rejection from others. People who develop perfectionism this way tend to apply this behaviour in selected situations and towards certain people. They may display perfectionistic thinking and behaviour at work but not at home; or over-please their employer but not their partner. They will channel this effort in situations that they view as critical to meeting their needs and obtaining recognition, and in people that they feel threatened or intimidated by.

Trying to maintain 'the perfect life' requires a lot of energy and commitment. It is therefore not surprising that people with high perfectionistic traits become seriously ill both physically and psychologically. Not only that, they live a very unhappy life, and struggle to maintain healthy relationships. Their life consists of all work and no play. What maintains this pattern of behaviour is their constant need for acceptance and praise from others, hence their continuous strive for achievement. They will often over-please and over-commit to others in the hope that their efforts will be appreciated. Unfortunately, they also believe that everyone should be like them and return the same respect and effort, only to become very disappointed when it is not.

This can reinforce the cycle of over-pleasing and over-committing especially when this is directed at toxic people who may be prone to taking advantage of this. When they feel that someone has let them down or have taken advantage of them, they become resentful towards that person, and extremely hurt. Their behaviour can even become very reactive and irrational and can come across confusing to those who are oblivious to what has been 'brewing behind the scenes", and may not have intentionally wanted to upset them. Unfortunately, most people will accept what you do for them if they assume that you are doing it because it brings you pleasure. For example,

> *Helen welcomes her new neighbour and clicks with her immediately, they have the same interests, and she's friendly etc. They spend a lot of time together and Helen feels like they have connected. Her new neighbour asks Helen to baby- sit her two young children as she needs to work and Helen agrees to do this. Four months go by and Helen does everything to make sure she does not let her new friendly neighbour down. She feeds her kids as an additional favour to same her neighbour time. One day Helen is not able to baby-sit as she has an important appointment to attend and tried everything to change it but was not able to do so. She tells her neighbour that she will not be able to baby-sit her children and even though she gives her plenty of notice, her neighbour behaves aggressively towards Helen and tells her that she has let her down. Helen at first feels very guilty*

until she realises after talking to others she realises that her neighbour's behaviour was unwarranted. She then feels very angry towards her neighbour as she realises that she has been taken for granted and that the relationship was one sided all this time. She ends the relationship and grieves the loss of that friendship and all the 'wasted time she dedicated towards it'. Helen feels unvalued and worthless and cannot believe that yet another person in her life has taken advantage of her and not valued her.

This is typical behaivour of a perfectionist. The more they over-please and the less they receive in return, the more they feel unvalued and unworthy. The more unvalued and unworthy they feel, the stronger their need to over-please. In order to break this cycle, they need to address the underlying cause of their over-pleasing behaviour – their poor sense of self-worth and the cognitive distortions that are maintaining this behaviour.

Attaching self-worth to achievements can only have a harmful effect on your psychological well-being. If you permit yourself to only feel worthy whenever you achieve something and unworthy when you do not, then you may put unnecessary pressure on yourself to continuously strive to achieve just so you can maintain a high sense of self-worth. Diagram 6.1 demonstrates this concept. That would be all well and good, if it was actually possible to have total control over all the factors that contribute to the success of an outcome. Perfectionists believe that they have one hundred percent control over all outcomes that they set out to achieve, and therefore, take one hundred percent credit for successful outcomes and one hundred percent blame for failed ones.

DIAGRAM 6.1

Attachment of Self-Worth to Achievements

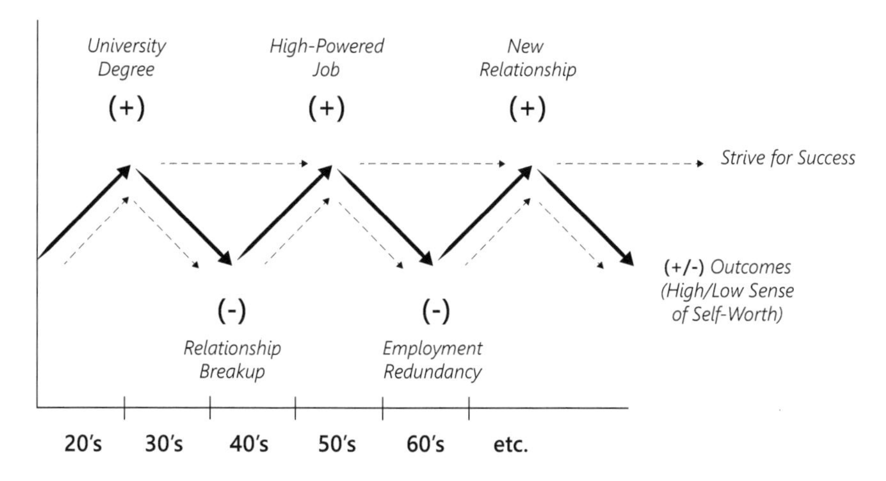

You might feel worthy when you achieve your university degree, and a job in the career you have chosen, but how worthy will you feel if you were made redundant from that job? Chances are that you will feel unworthy particularly, if you personalise that failed outcome. If you blame yourself for that redundancy it means that you have interpreted that outcome as your failure. However, what if you were not to blame for that failure? What if an external factor beyond your control was the contributing factor to that failed outcome and had nothing to do with you? For example, in my early twenties, I was made redundant from my position that I held for only three months. My manager, sat me down and told me that I was not to blame myself because the reason he was not able to keep me on was because sales had dropped due to the recession, and given that I was the last to come into the organisation, and therefore, the least experienced, it only made sense that I was the one chosen to be made redundant.

When I assessed this outcome in an objective manner and reflected on the three months of my employment, I accepted his explanation. During the three months of employment, I was never criticised about my performance, I managed to successfully complete my responsibilities in my role and meet my work deadlines, received compliments from both staff and customers, and noticed that the workload had decreased over the three months of my employment. Hence, losing my job was a failed outcome, but based on the evidence I collected, it would be unfair for me to think of myself as a failure in that instance. We learned in previous chapters how important it was to assess criticism by collecting objective evidence before drawing a conclusion on whether or not that criticism was justified. The same concept must be applied to both failed and successful outcomes.

INTERNAL VS EXTERNAL LOCUS OF CONTROL

A person's "locus" is conceptualised as either internal (the person believes they can control their life) or external (meaning they believe their decisions and life are controlled by environmental factors which they cannot influence, or by chance or fate).

Individuals with a strong internal locus of control believe events in their life derive primarily from their own actions: for example, when receiving exam results, people with an internal locus of control tend to praise or blame themselves and their abilities. People with a strong external locus of control tend to praise or blame external factors such as the teacher or the exam. Neither of these are healthy. Perfectionists tend to have a strong internal locus of control. They do not consider external factors that also play a contributing part in the outcome. For example, successfully completing a degree, Perfectionists believe that they are fully responsible for achieving the outcome and therefore will take full credit. However, if they fail, they will also take full blame. When assessing the contributing factors to either a failed or successful outcome, you need to consider all possible factors that played a contributing role in the outcome, that you actually had control over, and that you did not have control over.

For example, if you were fired from your job, before coming to the conclusion that you have failed, you would need to take into account all the factors that you had control over and all the factors you did not have control over that outcome. The factors that you have had control over may include, being punctual, not missing a day off work, asking for clarification on anything you weren't sure of, picking the job up quickly, following instructions correctly et cetera. The factors that you might not have had control over may include, whether you were given the full training you were promised, whether the expectations for that position was realistic, if you had sufficient resources to work with et cetera.

Diagram 6.2 demonstrates this concept. You may have only had 80% control over that outcome but it was the 20% that you did not have any control over that contributed to that failure. Without the training level that was promised to you during the interview, you were not able to perform the level of standard required by the employer at the expected timeframe. So who failed who? In this particular example, it appears that the boss has let you down by not providing the necessary training that you were promised at the interview, and as a result you did not have all the information needed to perform the task expected of you.

DIAGRAM 6.2

80%	**INTERNAL CONTROL** *(Factors controlled by the person)* • Being punctual • Committing to the job • Having a strong learning ability • Asking for assistance when needed • Depending on the skills you already have • Listening and following instructions carefully
20%	**EXTERNAL CONTROL** *(Factors not in the person's control)* • Level of training given • Level of expectation in learning by the manager • Available resources to acquire expected level of experience and knowledge of the job

A parent may have control over their parenting style and guidance in how well their child develops, however, they do not have control over that child's personality nor the external influences such as, friends, other family members, teachers et cetera.

A partner may have control over their relationship, in that they can communicate with them openly, be affectionate, attentive, responsible, loving, understanding, honest, and trustworthy, however, they do not have control over their partner's true feelings towards them, or whether they return the same towards them, nor do they have control over their partner's mental health, personality or external influences.

A person may have some control in successfully learning to play the piano, in that they can listen to instructions intently, put a lot of effort in the practice, however, they do not have control over the fact that they may not have the capacity to pick it up naturally because they may not have the creative ability to have that ear for music.

Is it your fault if you do not have the skills, experience, knowledge, or qualities for instance, to learn something that may come more naturally to someone else? If that is a factor that you do not have control over, then how can you call yourself a failure. You might fail at something that you do not have control over, but you will succeed at the things that you do have control over. Everyone has their own strengths and weaknesses, your weakness may be a strength in someone else, however, your strength may be a weakness in that same person. Take credit and blame where it is deserved and what determines this is the degree of control you have over something or someone's behaviour in that situation.

In the same way that it is important to consider the contributing factors to either a negative or positive outcome, it is equally important that prior to committing to a task or responsibility that the degree of control needed to achieve a positive outcome, be first identified. Working out the internal and external factors that influence the outcome is extremely important in maintaining an accurate conclusion/judgment of one's successes and failures. In the same way that you should not blame yourself for something that you did not have control over, you should also accept blame for something you did have control over. If you lost your job because you did not pay attention, or you were not punctual, or lied about your skills or experiences, then you must accept the fact that you have failed and learn from it. Blaming others for your mistakes or blaming yourself for someone else's mistakes is not being fair or responsible. Remember, that identifying and accepting your strengths and weaknesses is a vital part in developing a healthy and genuine sense of identity and worth.

Achievements are only opportunities that demonstrate your skills, qualities, experiences, knowledge and capabilities – the true attributes that make you the worthy person you are. Achievements should not be used to measure your sense of worth.

CHANGING COGNITIVE DISTORTIONS

Below is a list of typical Cognitive Distortions of people with rigid, perfectionistic thinking and behaviour.

1. 'ALL OR NOTHING' THINKING

They see things in black and white categories (ie., with no middle ground). Eg., If their performance falls short of perfect, they see themselves as a complete failure. They will only attempt activities that they are sure they will succeed 100%.

2. OVER GENERALISATION

They see a single negative event as a never ending, 'spreading' constant pattern of defeat. Eg., If they make a mistake, they will interpret this as failure.

3. DISCOUNTING THE POSITIVE

They reject positive experiences by insisting 'they don't count' for some reason or another and focus only on the negative experiences.

4. JUMPING TO CONCLUSIONS

They make a negative interpretation even though there are no definite facts to support their conclusion (mind reading and 'fortune telling' errors).

5. MAGNIFICATION OR MINIMISATION

They turn things into catastrophe by exaggerating the importance of some things (such as making a mistake/an achievement), or they shrink things until they appear tiny (their own good qualities or someone else's imperfections). This is also called the 'binocular trick'.

6. EMOTIONAL REASONING

They assume that their negative emotions necessarily reflect the way things really are (I feel it, therefore, it must be true!).

7. SHOULD STATEMENTS

They try to motivate themselves with 'shoulds', 'musts' and 'oughts'. The emotional consequence is guilt. When they direct 'should' statements toward others, they feel anger, frustration and resentment.

8. LABELING

This is an extreme form of over generalising. Instead of describing an error, they attach a negative label, "I'm a loser"/'He's always been incompetent".

9. PERSONALISATION

They see themselves as the cause of some negative external event, which in fact, they are not primarily responsible for or even in control of.

SETTING REALISTIC STANDARDS

One of the necessary changes that a perfectionist needs to make is to 'normalise' the standards they set out to achieve. Normalising means setting a realistic achievable standard. To normalise, one needs to collect external information and work out the average or normal standard based on the majority of the findings. Perfectionists set standards based on their own beliefs without first checking if their standards are what the majority of the target population achieves. For example, if you wanted to set up a private practice and you needed to determine how long it would take to achieve a full time practice, you would need to collect data from a sample group and work out the average timeframe that group took to build a fulltime private practice. If the 'norm' was two years, and if you achieved a full-time practice in one year then that could be considered as an achievement.

A perfectionist might instead, set the goal of building a successful private practice in six months and set out to achieve this, only to find it extremely difficult and push through to achieve this unrealistic deadline and experience a lot of unnecessary excessive stress, or not even be able to achieve it within six months and blame themselves for not achieving this goal. Similarly, if you are a mother of two children, living off campus and studying a university degree, it would make more sense for you to compare your marks against other mothers in a similar situation to yours rather than to compare your marks to students who are only responsible for themselves and who are living on campus and therefore have more time to study and more access to the university library and resources. Similarly, compare your appearance to your own age, why compare yourself to a twenty-year old when you are forty years old? Compare your household standard to the majority of people who also work full-time. How many times do they vacuum their carpet? What standard of cleanliness is the majority of homes that are occupied by people who work fulltime? Compare apples to apples, not apples to oranges and always set standards that are achievable and fair by collecting information from 'the majority' of similar situations, and base your standards on the average of that majority ('Normalise' your standards).

You can see how important it is to assess a situation in an objective manner to draw an accurate conclusion, especially when the information is to assess yourself as a person. We learned earlier in the piece how to apply this strategy of thinking to negative outcomes, criticisms and negative self-talk. This strategy is not only important in helping us recognise our true weaknesses, but also in recognising the qualities and skills that form part of our identity. In the following chapter you will learn how to apply the Objective Screening strategy to identify your qualities and skills - an important step in the formation of your identity.

CHAPTER SEVEN

RECOGNISING YOUR QUALITIES AND SKILLS

"You attract people by the qualities you display. You keep them by the qualities you possess." – Source Unknown.

PSYCHOLOGISTS most commonly use the term "identity" to describe personal identity, or the idiosyncratic things that make a person unique. It is who you think you are and how you perceive and define yourself.

SELF-ESTEEM AND FORMING AN IDENTITY

Developing self-esteem plays an important role in developing a strong sense of identity, and both important to good mental health and how you relate to others. Forming an identity without a healthy self-esteem is extremely difficult. As we learned earlier, having a strong sense of self-worth enables us to get what we want out of life, and this helps us to form our true identity. Having an understanding of our true weaknesses, and of our qualities and skills, will make it easier to seek from life what we want and need for a healthy and fulfilling life.

As we discovered earlier, the interpretations we form from both the negative and positive experiences we have determines how we perceive ourselves, and as we also learned, the accuracy of what we interpret is vital in the development of a healthy self-esteem and self-identity. Therefore, in the same way that we identified our true weaknesses by using the Objective Screening technique, we need to use this technique to identify the qualities and skills that form our true identity, and that differentiates us from others. Our perception of ourselves must consist of an accurate account of both our weaknesses and strengths – our Identity.

Diagram 7.1, 7.2, and 7.3, on the following pages provide examples, of how to apply the Objective Screening Technique to identify your qualities and skills.

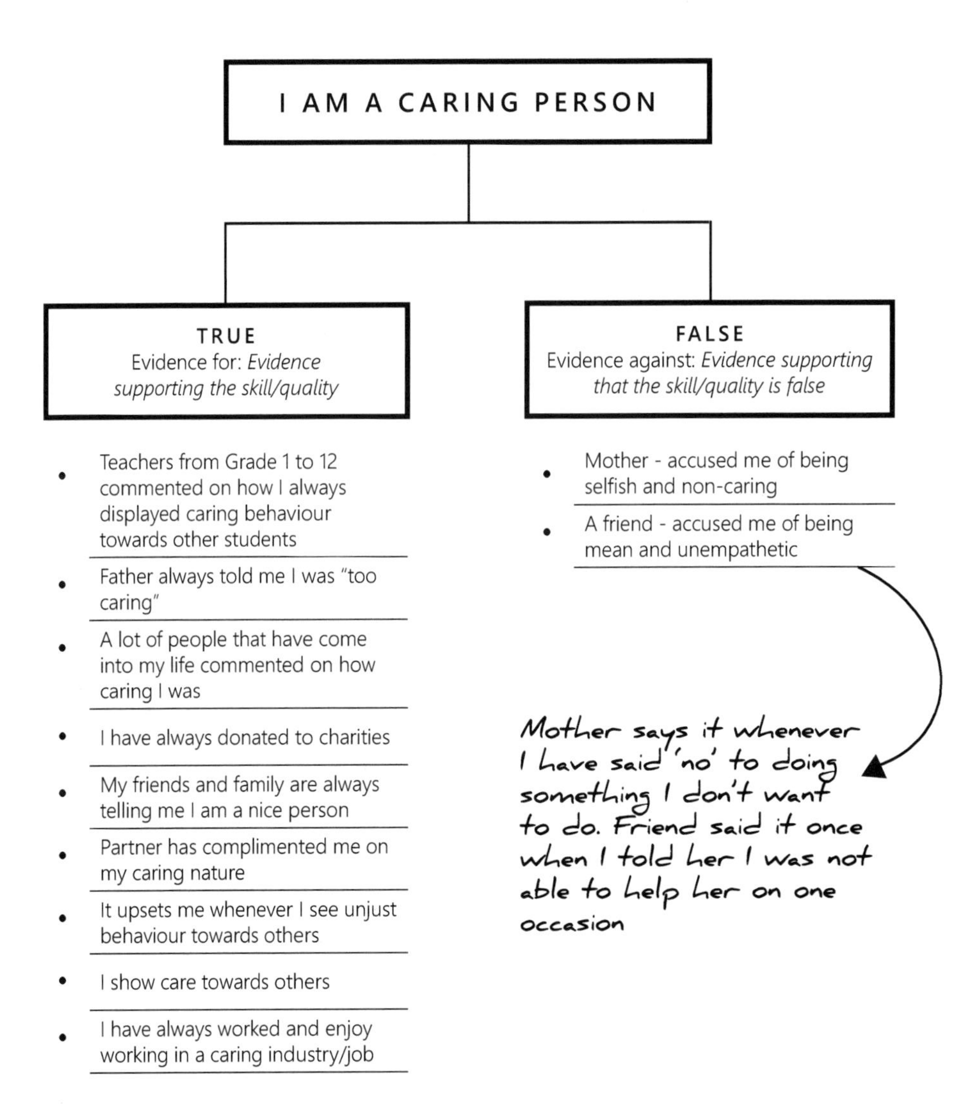

DIAGRAM 7.1: There is more objective evidence supporting the fact that being a caring person is a true quality.

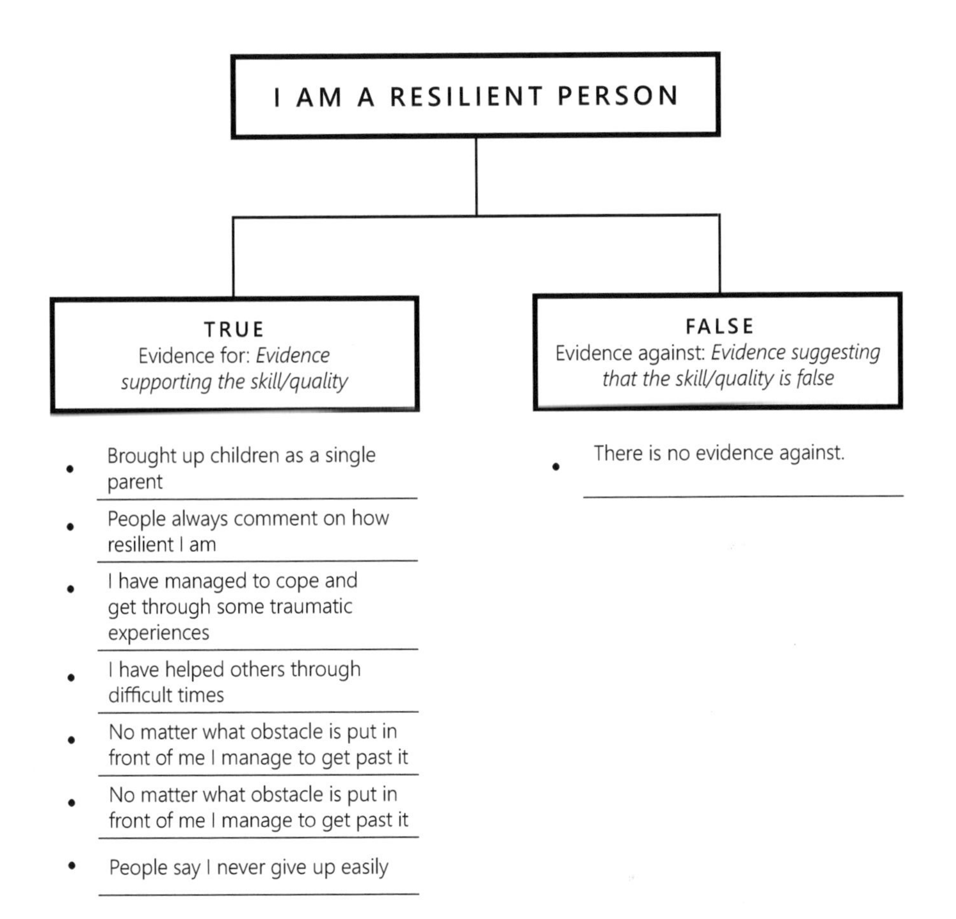

DIAGRAM 7.2: There is more objective evidence supporting the fact that being a resilient person is a true quality.

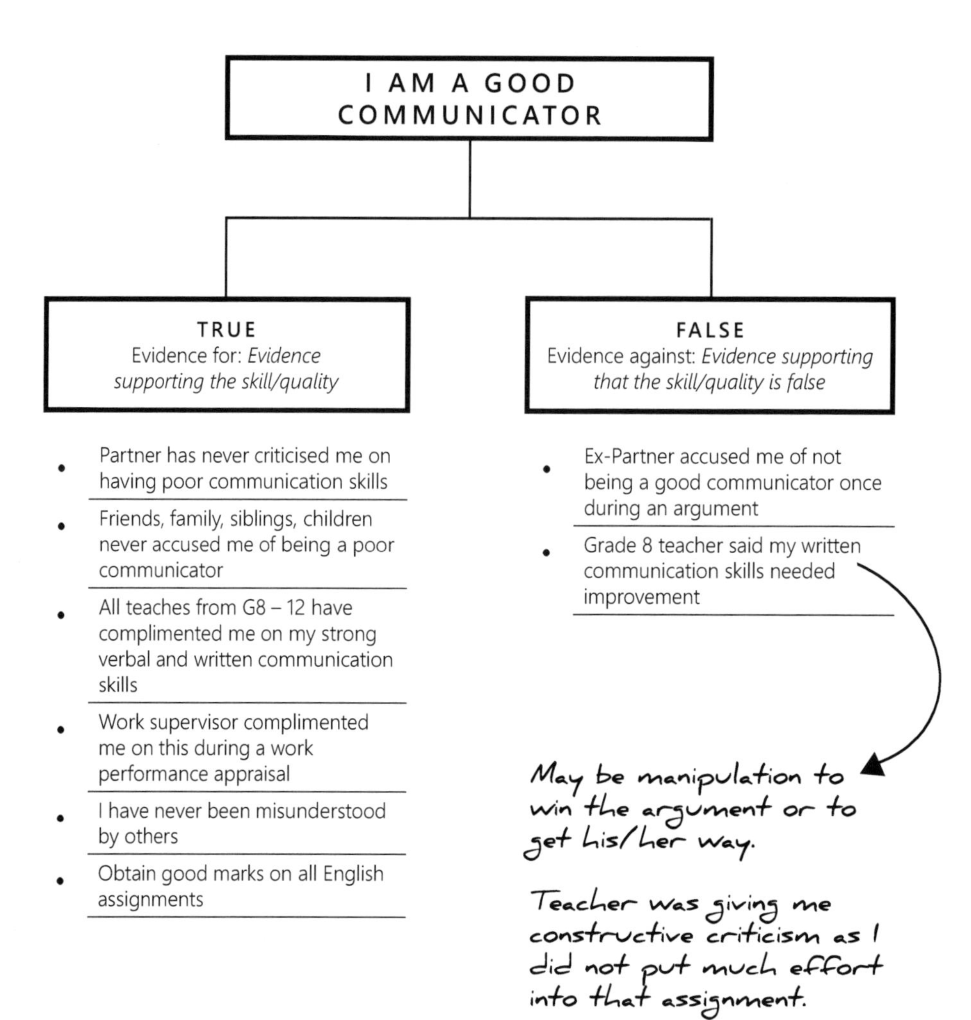

DIAGRAM 7.3: There is more objective evidence supporting the fact that being a good communicator is a true quality.

HOMEWORK

ACTIVITY 7A:

Below is a Checklist of Personal Skills and Characteristics. Using the Objective Screening template on Page 106 and 107, based on the objective evidence for and against that you have collected, tick off five characteristics and skills that describe you best. Note: Be mindful of not including what you think or feel as part of your evidence.

CHECKLIST OF PERSONAL SKILLS

The following words describe skills and characteristics.

- **Accurate:** Careful, precise, free from error.
- **Adaptable:** Able to adapt oneself to new surroundings; to make suitable change so as to fit new conditions.
- **Alert:** Watchful, wide awake, ready to act.
- **Ambitious:** Full of ambition, strong desire "to do" something.
- **Amiable:** Feeling and inspiring friendliness; lovable.
- **Analytical:** Employing analytic methods; separating things into their parts of elements.
- **Articulate:** Able to express oneself clearly, do not mumble.
- **Assertive:** Insist on one's rights or opinions.
- **Attentive:** To notice, pay attention to, careful attention.
- **Broad-minded:** Being tolerant or liberal in thought or opinion.
- **Businesslike:** Practical, systematic.
- **Calm:** Stillness, serenity, peaceful, undisturbed.
- **Capable:** Having the skills/ability or fitness for.
- **Careful:** Watchful, cautious, concerned for.
- **Competent:** Adequately qualified, ability.
- **Confident:** Trusting, fully assured, belief, trust in yourself.
- **Conscientious:** Good moral understanding of right and wrong.

- **Consistent:** Constant to same principles, not changing.
- **Cooperative:** Work well with others.
- **Dedicated:** Devoted to aims or vocation.
- **Dependable:** May be relied on.
- **Determined:** To do, resolve, on a course of action.
- **Efficient:** Competent, capable, able to get results.
- **Energetic:** Active, full of life, vigorous, an energetic worker.
- **Enterprising:** Strong interest, great eagerness.
- **Flexible:** Manageable, adaptable, versatile.
- **Hardworking:** Done with energy, industrious.
- **Honest:** Not lying, cheating or stealing, sincere.
- **Independent:** Ability to work on your own without being constantly supervised.
- **Industrious:** Hardworking, diligent.
- **Innovative:** Make changes, introduction of something new.
- **Motivated:** The inner reason for any act; as, hunger might be the motive for working.
- **Optimistic:** View that good prevails over evil.
- **Organised:** Place things in working order.
- **Patient:** Calm.
- **People-oriented:** Enjoy working/being with people.
- **Persevering:** Steadfast pursuit to an aim, refusal to give up; continued effort.
- **Practical:** Inclined or suited to useful action, rather that speculation.
- **Productive:** Tending to produce.
- **Realistic:** Practical views/policy, truth/detail, presenting people/ scenes as they are.
- **Reliable:** Dependable.
- **Resourceful:** Ability to supply what is needed, quick wit.
- **Responsible:** Capable of rational conduct, trustworthy.
- **Versatile:** Turning easily or readily from occupation/job to another, changeable.

- **Communicate:** Speak and/or write well and get your ideas across to other easily.
- **Interpret:** Look at things and make sense of them, figure out what makes things work and why there is a problem, etc.
- **Analyse:** Break a problem down to see what is really going on.
- **Creativity:** Use your imagination to come up with new ideas or to solve problems.
- **Order Goods/Supplies:** Keep track of items and how to order them.
- **Decision Making:** Make good judgements about what to do in a difficult situation, even when the supervisor is not present.
- **Adapt to Situations:** Learn a new task and/or work in a different area with different co- workers.
- **Explain:** Tell others why you do certain things the way you do or why you think the way you do.
- **Think Ahead:** Plan your day and keep problems/accidents from happening.
- **Calculate Numbers:** Use a calculator, cash register or computer to answer numerical questions.
- **Operate Equipment:** Turn equipment on and off as well as how to use it safely and wisely. (If you don't know how to operate certain things, you always ask for help.)
- **Record Data:** Write thorough and accurate notes/numbers.
- **Set Goals:** Set goals for yourself to achieve and plan ways to achieve them.
- **Learn Quickly:** Do new things and carry out new responsibilities easily by watching other or by following instructions.
- **Confident:** Believe in and feel good about yourself.
- **Pleasant:** Nice person for others to talk to and be with.
- **Energetic:** Lots of energy to use at work and at play.
- **Helpful:** Enjoy helping people solve their problems.
- **Trustworthy:** Can be trusted to get the job done, to look after things or keep secrets that are very important to other people.
- **Efficient:** Perform tasks in the fastest and simplest ways that they can be done.
- **Organise:** Arrange people/plan events/put things in order so that they run smoothly.

- **Delegate:** Assign tasks to others to complete.
- **Assemble Products:** Put things together with your hands.
- **Take Instructions:** Follow instructions well, ask questions when you do not fully understand instructions.
- **Motivate Others:** Help keep others' spirits up and encourage them to do their best.
- **Service Customers:** Be friendly, patient and polite with customers and try your best to service their needs/wants.
- **Dependable:** Can be counted on to do what you said you would do (i.e. show up for work on time, do your job duties well, etc.).
- **Flexible:** Can carry out many different responsibilities, sometimes with very little advanced notice.
- **Self-assured:** Feel very confident and positive about yourself and your abilities.
- **Supervise:** Watch others to make sure that everything is ok and/or that they are doing their jobs well.
- **Time Management:** Plan your time so that you don't forget to do things, you're almost always/always on time, and you know how to prioritise and give yourself enough time to do the things that you need to do.
- **Trouble-shoot:** Figure out what the problem is, why there is a problem, or prevent a problem before it happens.
- **Handle Complaints:** Deal effectively with complaints made by customers or constructive criticism from your employer.
- **Listen:** Listen/pay attention to what others are saying, without daydreaming or forming judgement about them.
- **Considerate:** Always think about how others may feel about things, especially before you say or do things that my affect them.
- **Punctual:** Always on time for things.
- **Loyal:** Committed and devoted to things/people that mean a lot to you (i.e. your best friend, your job/supervisor).
- **Precise:** Make sure that things are done accurately, correctly and exactly.
- **Resourceful:** Thing of new, creative and different ways to do things when there are no obvious solutions available.

(http://www.ceswoodstock.org) (See Appendix A - Objective Screening Exercise)

OBJECTIVE SCREENING TECHNIQUE

By applying the Objective Screening Technique to past negative criticism that you are still hanging on to, you will eventually 'clean that filter'. By applying the technique to incoming criticism and negative thoughts, you will maintain "that clean filter' and therefore, maintain a healthy self-esteem. This technique will take some practice to master and to become a natural habit of thinking, but once it does, your self-esteem can only strengthen overtime. Developing essential problem-solving skills and assertiveness skills are also important in having a healthy self-esteem, and this will be covered in the following chapters of this book.

HOMEWORK

TRUE Evidence for: *Evidence supporting the criticism*	FALSE Evidence against: *Evidence supporting that the criticism is false*
•	•
•	•
•	•
•	•
•	•
•	•
•	•
•	•
•	•
•	•
•	•
•	•
•	•
•	•
•	•
•	•

HOMEWORK

TRUE Evidence for: *Evidence supporting the criticism*	FALSE Evidence against: *Evidence supporting that the criticism is false*
• ______	• ______
• ______	• ______
• ______	• ______
• ______	• ______
• ______	• ______
• ______	• ______
• ______	• ______
• ______	• ______
• ______	• ______
• ______	• ______
• ______	• ______
• ______	• ______
• ______	• ______
• ______	• ______
• ______	• ______
• ______	• ______

CHAPTER EIGHT

PROACTIVE PROBLEM-SOLVING SKILLS

"Running away from any problem only increases the distance from the solution. The easiest way to escape from the problem is to solve it" – Unknown Author.

PEOPLE who are susceptible to Anxiety and/or Depression commonly respond to situations in a reactive, rather than proactive manner and will readjust their response accordingly only after they have analysed the situation. Proactive problem solving involves the process of assessing the severity of the situation, the risk or potential for that situation to occur, and the impact/loss that the 'worst case scenario' will bring on should it happen.

REACTIVE PROBLEM-SOLVING VS PROACTIVE PROBLEM-SOLVING

Reactive Problem-Solving Steps:

1. Situation (-)

2. Emotional/Physical Response

3. Assessment of the Situation

4. Adjustment of Emotional/Physical Response.

When a negative situation triggers a realistic or unrealistic fear and you do not first assess the situation, and you respond to the situation in an emotionally reactive way, you are likely to activate your adrenal response prematurely. If the situation does not warrant such a reaction, you are likely to experience the anxiety symptoms explained earlier. This may continue for a while until either you realise that the situation was not as bad as you originally thought it was, or when the situation is eventually resolved. In which case, the reaction might have been more than necessary.

For example, if you hear a rumour that the organisation you are working for is going to make certain positions redundant, you might start to panic and continue to panic until you eventually find out that your position is safe. You might have panicked unnecessarily for days, weeks or months. Pressing the 'panic button' prematurely without first assessing the likelihood of the worst case occurring, and of the severity of the outcome should it occur, will only result in you experiencing excessive worrying, and possibly anxiety symptoms.

It is therefore crucial to always assess the situation thoroughly so that your response will be as it should be. While it is normal for you to respond to some situations by releasing a certain level of Adrenalin to help you deal with the situation effectively and efficiently, it is not a normal response for your system to be 'flooded' with Adrenalin that is only going to make dealing with the situation more difficult.

Proactive Problem-Solving Steps

1. Situation (-) Real/Unrealistic

2. Assessment of the Situation

3. Emotional/Physical Response.

Using the example provided above, if you hear a rumour that the organisation you are working for is going to make certain positions redundant, you should first collect as much information as you can to help you determine the likelihood that your position may be one of them by perhaps seeking information from your manager to clarify this for you. Once you have this information and you realise that your position is safe, or that there is a low risk of it being made redundant, you still want to analyse how bad your situation would be should you actually lose your position. You can do this by collecting information such as, the length of time your redundancy payout is likely to carry you financially while you are looking for another job, the savings you have in your bank account, the length of time you think it will take you to find another similar job given the demand for your experience and skill et cetera. Depending on the information you collect will determine the amount of Adrenalin you will need to have to work through the solution. The amount of Adrenalin being released will be the correct dosage needed to achieve this. Assessing the situation first will help you to work out quickly if your fear of the worst case is actually real or unrealistic/catastrophised, and prevent any unnecessary over-reaction.

Unrealistic Fear: What If?

What if? = What is the chance of this happening? (Low, Medium, High) + What is the impact or consequence or loss that it will cause you should it happen? (Low, Medium, High).

Based on the objective information you collect, determine the gravity of the situation and likelihood of it occurring. Respond according to the outcome that you expect from your assessment findings.

You will find it may take you some time to break your bad habits of thinking, and that you might initially have to apply the new approach even after you may have already dealt with a situation using your old habit. Applying the new approach, even after you have already dealt with a situation using the wrong approach is still practice. In time, this new approach in dealing with situations will occur automatically. Below is a couple of examples of how to deal with fear that is brought on by catastrophic thinking.

Scenario 1: You hear a rumour that the organisation you are working for is merging and looking at making some positions redundant. The worst case scenario comes to mind and your levels of anxiety are high.

What If formula:

a. Analyse the information you have available to you that is the objective and factual. Do not include what you assume, think or feel is going on. Only what is actually going on based on the objective information you have to work with.

b. If you do not have sufficient information, then you need to collect that information straight from the horse's mouth, the people who have the power to make these changes.

c. Once you have all the possible facts, then adjust the risk of the situation happening. If you are informed that your department is safe, then the risk is low if not nil. If you are informed that there are certain positions within your department that may be made redundant, then the risk is medium. If on the other-hand you are informed that all positions within your department is going to be made redundant then the risk is high. However, if you do not have any information to determine the 'risk factor' to adjust your guard accordingly, you are best to channel your energy towards adjusting to the changes and/or impact that may be brought about if it actually occurs.

RISK: (No factual information) = ***Nil/low degree.***

RISK: (Some factual information) = ***Medium degree.***

RISK: (Strong factual information) = ***High degree.***

d. Once you have determined the Risk the next step is to determine the Impact that the situation is expected to have on you and your life. That is how much is that situation actually going to affect you. To do this you will need to think of the worst case scenario based again only on objective facts and not on what you think or feel might happen.

IMPACT: (No factual information) = ***Nil/Low degree.***

IMPACT: (No factual Information) = ***Medium degree.***

IMPACT: (Strong factual information) = ***High degree.***

What If: *Risk (Medium-High) + Impact (Nil/Low) = Mild Levels of Adrenalin (enough to slightly increase your alertness and guard to deal with the situation effectively and efficiently).*

If the Risk is medium to high, that is there is a chance that your position may be made redundant, but you did a job search and found that there are a number of similar positions available to apply for if it came to this, you have savings in your bank account that may be able to carry you for three months, your partner's income will be sufficient for living expenses for three to six months, your skills and experience are specialised and may be well looked upon by potential employers, you have past experience or skills you can fall back on if needed, your redundancy package may be sufficient to carry you financially for twelve months, et cetera, then the impact on you and your life should be low if not nil.

If on the other-hand the facts indicate a medium-high Impact, worrying excessively will do nothing to prevent it from happening, and therefore, you are best to utilise your energy into looking at all your options and working out a solution that you will be inevitably forced to do regardless.

What if: *Risk (Medium-High) + Impact (Medium-High) = Adrenalin levels should be at a higher level to enable you to urgently seek alternative employment and to weight up your best options, but not high enough to cause you unnecessary anxiety that will only make it more difficult for you to get through this process.*

Adrenalin that is released by your system is to help you, not hinder you. However, if more Adrenalin is released than is necessary (typically by catastrophic thinking), your body will instead 'freeze up' and exhibit symptoms of Anxiety that will interfere with effective problem-solving.

HOMEWORK

HOMEWORK 8A:

Apply the 'What if" formula to situations in the past that you may have responded to in an over-reactive manner.

Exercise 1: *What If Exercise*

What if (situation):

____

____

____

____

____

What is the likelihood of that this situation will occur? (collect objective information, do not rely on what you think or feel).

____

____

____

____

____

[Low] / [Medium] / [High]

How much of an impact will it have on you should it occur? (collect objective information, do not rely on what you think or feel).

____

____

____

____

____

[Low] / [Medium] / [High]

(See Appendix B - What If Exercise)

CHAPTER NINE

ASSERTIVENESS AND SETTING BOUNDARIES

"You must recognise your rights and stand up for them. If you do not other people define your role for you and you stop being yourself. " – Herbert Fensterheim.

THERE would be very few people who, at some time in their lives have not been in a situation where they wish they had been able to respond differently. Sometimes these situations involve saying no or making a request. At other times it may involve responding to criticism or giving 'constructive' criticism. It may even involve giving or receiving compliments. It is in many of these situations that assertiveness is useful and appropriate.

WHAT IS ASSERTIVENESS?

1. Recognising and expressing needs, feelings and opinions, negative and positive.
2. Asking clearly and directly for what you want.
3. Saying 'no' politely and establishing boundaries.
4. Letting go of old patterns of behaviour, unrewarding relationships and situations.
5. Taking responsibility for your feelings and actions, and using "I" statements.
6. Respecting yourself: listening to what your body is telling you.
7. Respecting other people and listening to them.
8. Being prepared to compromise to resolve conflict.
9. Setting goals and planning steps to achieve them.
10. Empowering others and wanting them to be happy.

Assertiveness thus involves standing up for personal rights and expressing thoughts, feelings and beliefs, in direct, honest and appropriate ways, which do not violate another person's rights. Now that we have an idea of what Assertion is, it is important to be aware of the other ways that we sometimes respond. One of these methods is **Aggression**.

Agressiveness Is directly standing up for personal rights and expressing thoughts, feelings and beliefs in a way which is often dishonest, usually inappropriate, and always violates the rights of others.

The usual goal of aggression is domination and winning. Winning is insured by humiliating, degrading, belittling, or overpowering other people so that they become weaker and less able to express their needs and rights.

Alternatively.......

Non Assertion/Passive Behaviour Involves failing to express honest feelings, thoughts, and beliefs and consequently permitting another person to violate or abuse oneself, or expressing ones feelings in such an apologetic, diffident, self-effacing manner, that others can easily disregard them.

It shows lack of respect for one's own needs. The goal of non-assertive behaviour is to appease others and to avoid conflict at any cost.

ASSERTIVE PEOPLE ARE:

Direct	*Honest*	*Specific*
Risk Taking	*Challenging*	*Initiating*
Equal	*Caring*	*Non-judgemental*
Clear	*Spontaneous*	*Self-aware*

Assertive People:

- Use 'I' Statements and take responsibility for their actions
- Listen attentively
- Ask for what they want.
- Refuse what they don't want.
- Exercise choice, make decisions.
- Listen to criticism and accept or reject it.
- Accept compliments.
- Acknowledge and praise other people's qualities and achievements
- Accept that other people have limitations
- Express positive and negative feelings
- Have a healthy level of self-esteem
- Enjoy today and set goals for tomorrow

Assertive People do not:

- Beat around the bush
- Go behind people's backs
- Bully
- Call people names
- Bottle up their feelings.

Assertiveness is:

- Recognising and expressing needs, feelings and opinions, negative and positive.
- Asking clearly and directly for what you want.
- Saying 'no' politely and establishing boundaries.
- Letting go of old patterns of behaviour, unrewarding relationships and situations.
- Taking responsibility for your feelings and actions, and using 'I' statements.
- Respecting yourself: listening to what your body is telling you.
- Respecting other people and listening to them.
- Being prepared to compromise to resolve conflict.
- Setting goals and planning steps to achieve them.
- Empowering others and wanting them to be happy.

Assertiveness thus involves standing up for personal rights and expressing thoughts, feelings and beliefs, in direct, honest and appropriate ways, which do not violate another person's rights. It involves respect for one's self and another person's needs and rights.

Assertiveness is an alternative to passive, aggressive and manipulative behaviour.

Before you can begin to become 'assertive' it is important to fully understand the difference between an aggressive and assertive response. Many people confuse assertion with aggression and many people fear becoming assertive because they fear confrontation should they come across an aggressive person. The one important thing to remember is that someone who behaves aggressively is someone who is highly likely to be insecure and have poor self-confidence.

WHAT IS AGGRESSIVE BEHAVIOUR?

Now that you have an idea of what Assertion is, it is important to be aware of the other ways that we sometimes respond. One of these methods is **Aggression.**

Aggressiveness is directly standing up for personal rights and expressing thoughts, feelings and beliefs in a way which is often **dishonest, usually inappropriate,** and always **violates the rights of others.** The usual goal of aggression is domination and winning. Winning is insured by **humiliating, degrading, belittling, or overpowering** other people so that they become weaker and less able to express their needs and rights.

Alternatively ......

Non Assertion or **Passivity** involves **failing** to express **honest feelings, thoughts, and beliefs** and consequently permitting another person to violate or abuse oneself, or expressing one's feelings in such an **apologetic, diffident, self-effacing** manner that others can easily disregard them. It shows **lack of respect** for **one's own needs.** The goal of non-assertion is to **satisfy** others and to **avoid conflict** at any cost.

WHY BOTHER TO BE ASSERTIVE?

Assertive behaviour often leads to compromise and negotiation rather than an outright win for one party only. Manipulative, 'behind the back' techniques and aggressive behaviour may get us more of what we want in terms of material goods or power more often but usually at great expense to our personal relationships and self-esteem. More often assertion will prevent us from continually leaving situations feeling bad about ourselves and instead will leave us with a satisfaction that we 'did our best' and did so without abusing the rights of another person.

Assertive people are aware of both their strengths and weaknesses. They are not afraid of taking risks and know that by doing so they will probably make many mistakes. They also view mistakes positively and see them as an opportunity to learn and do better next time.

ACTIVITY

ACTIVITY 9A:

Identify different responses (ie., aggressive, unassertive or assertive) for each of the following scenarios. The answers are on the next page:

SCENARIO 1: *Mary is asked by telephone to be in charge of a charitable campaign in her neighbourhood. This is a responsibility she does not want to accept. She responds by saying, "I really don't want to take on that responsibility this year".*

[Unassertive]   [Aggressive]   [Assertive]

SCENARIO 2: *A friend is talking on and on, and Sue has to get dinner. She responds by telling her son to go ring the doorbell. Then saying, "I've got to hang up now. Someone's at the door".*

[Unassertive]   [Aggressive]   [Assertive]

SCENARIO 3: *John is seated in the window seat on an aeroplane during a business trip. A honeymooning couple in the seats beside him are waiting for everyone to leave before getting up. He has to connect with another plane. He responds by saying "Are you two every going to leave this plane?"*

[Unassertive]   [Aggressive]   [Assertive]

SCENARIO 4: *Angie is not pleased with the service in the restaurant. She responds by saying "I don't feel that I was given adequate service".*

[Unassertive]   [Aggressive]   [Assertive]

SCENARIO 5: *Vanessa's husband has not been helping her clean up the dishes after they have had guests for dinner. She responds by saying with sarcasm: "I just love to wait on you and your friends. It's my life's ambition".*

[Unassertive]   [Aggressive]   [Assertive]

SCENARIO 6: *Jody's male friend arrives to pick her up for a date thirty minutes later. They have missed the first part of the movie they planned to see. Jody responds by saying nothing, not even hello, as they drive to the movie.*

[Unassertive]   [Aggressive]   [Assertive]

ANSWERS:

S1.	Assertive	S4.	Assertive
S2.	Unassertive	S5.	Aggressive
S3.	Aggressive	S6.	Unassertive

ACTIVITY

ACTIVITY 9B:

Circle the characteristics in all categories that you believe you possess.

My Assessment of My Behaviour:

Passive	Aggressive	Indirect	Assertive
Vague	demanding	judgmental	use 'I' statements
Subservient	uncompromising	manipulative	state needs directly
Inhibited	arrogant	deceitful	honest
Self-pitying	blaming	blaming indirectly	accept blame
Avoidance	refuse to listen	half listen	responsible
Put self-down	put others down (to their face)	put others down (behind their backs)	respect self and others
Wanting	taking	taking indirectly	initiating
Loser	hurtful	reacting	forgiving
Ineffectual (don't make things happen)	pushy	pressurising	effective
Cowardly	loud	emotional bribery	spontaneous
Victim	winner	martyr (suffering for great cause)	realist
Powerless	power over	powerless	power within
I don't mind	dis-empowering	I don't mind	empowering

Everyone at some time has to cope with a problem. Two basic instinctual responses when encountering a problem are **flight** (passivity) and **fight** (aggressive). Many mental health and relationship problems are caused by an over-reliance on these two basic instinctual responses. There is a third (learned) response which is more appropriate and successful in solving these problems that is, **assertiveness**. Assertiveness involves **discussing, arguing,** and **negotiating**.

Assertive, Aggressive & Unassertive Behaviour

ASSERTIVE	AGGRESSIVE	UNASSERTIVE
	YOU DON'T:	
• Violate other people's rights • Expect other people to guess what you want • Freeze with anxiety.	• Respect that other people have a right to get their needs being met • Look for situations which you both might be able to get what you want.	• Ask for what you want • Express your feelings • Usually get what you want • Upset anyone • Get noticed.
	YOU DO:	
• Ask for what you want • Directly and openly • Appropriately • Have rights • Ask confidently and without necessary anxiety.	• Try to get what you want • In any way that works • Often gives rise to bad feelings in others • Threaten, cajole, manipulate, use sarcasm, fight.	• Hope to get what you want • By sitting on your feelings • Rely on others to guess what you want

PERSONAL RIGHTS

You Have Rights!

The first thing you need to know about how to become more assertive is your rights and your responsibilities to others. Experts would say that in our relationships with other people we are bound to have expectations of them. For example, we expect our friends to behave considerately. We have a right to such reasonable expectations. We don't however have a right to unreasonable expectations such as, a person giving up a cherished pastime for us! One of the best ways to make sure that our expectation of others is reasonable is to allow others the same rights as we expect for ourselves.

The Rights listed on the next page may seem quite ordinary and acceptable when you first read them, but it can take a long time for some of these rights to sink in, and for you to accept them for yourself, as well as for other people. Many people have little difficulty in accepting these rights for others, but the way they lead their lives shows that they do not accept them for themselves.

For example, we can be overly tolerant and quick to make excuses for others:

> *"She probably didn't realise..."*

But we don't always make those same excuses about ourselves!

> *"I'm 40 years old. You'd think I'd have learned by now..."*

While it may be difficult at first to accept you have these rights, not doing so will only lead to passive behaviour. Not expecting others to accord you these rights can allow them to behave aggressively towards you. You may need to return to this section and read it again, or to remind yourself of your rights from time to time, before you can begin fully to accept your own ability to allow yourself and other people these rights.

ACTIVITY

ACTIVITY 9:

Look at the lists on pages 127 and 128. These are your rights and you are entitled to them. Put a cross next to the rights you currently deny yourself and a tick against the rights you would benefit most from adopting.

My rights as a person

1. I have the right to be treated with respect as an equal human
2. I have the right to being whatever my perceived role or status in life.
3. I have the right to state my own needs and ask for what I want.
4. I have the right to define my own limits, look after my needs and say 'No'.
5. I have the right to express my feelings and opinions.
6. I have the right to ask for time to think before I agree, disagree or make a decision.
7. I have the right to make my own decisions.
8. I have the right to reconsider and change my mind.
9. I have the right to say 'I don't understand' and ask for clarification or help.
10. I have the right to make mistakes without feeling guilty or being made to feel foolish.
11. I have the right to hold my own values.
12. I have the right to be listened to when I speak.
13. I have the right to refuse responsibility for other people's problems if I so choose.
14. I have the right to set my own goals in life and strive to fulfil my own expectations as against the goals and expectations specified for me by others.
15. I have the right to relate to people without being dependent on them for approval.

Responsibilities in relation to rights

- I recognise that I have responsibilities as well as rights.
- I give other people the same rights that I give to myself.

Personal Rights in the Workplace

1. I have the right to be treated with respect whatever my position or status.
2. I have the right to say 'No' to requests that I consider are unreasonable or that I believe I cannot fulfill.
3. I have the right to ask for extra time to complete a task.
4. I have the right to ask for time to consider a request.
5. I have the right to be consulted on matters that affect me or my staff.
6. I have the right to be heard by my manager, my staff, and my colleagues.
7. I have the right to make occasional mistakes.
8. I have the right to ask for assistance and advice.
9. I have the right to training and opportunity to develop existing skills and learn new ones.
10. I have the right to receive credit and acknowledgment for my achievements at work.
11. I have the right to take care of myself and have sick leave or compassionate leave without feeling guilty or pressured.
12. I have the right to give constructive criticism to staff about performance or behaviour.
13. I have the right to fulfill my potential.

Responsibilities in relation to rights

- I have the responsibility to fulfill my contractual obligations and the duties within my job description.

HOW TO BECOME ASSERTIVE

ASSERTIVE BEHAVIOUR:

1. **Know what you want to say:** You won't appear confident if you are unsure of what you want. You could appear foolish by asking for something that you eventually realise is not what you want.
2. **Say it:** Don't hesitate or beat around the bush, come right out with it! Practice before you say it and check for appropriateness.
3. **Be specific:** Say exactly what you want or don't want, so that there can be no confusion. Begin with the word "I". No long explanations are necessary.
4. **Say it as soon as possible:** Do not let too much time pass, as this builds up apprehension. On the other hand, do not say it at the peak of your anger. Wait for your anger to pass.
5. **Look the person in the eye:** People feel more comfortable if you look directly at them. You simply look shifty if you cannot look them in the eye. You certainly will not come across as someone who knows what they want.
6. **Look relaxed:** You will convey anxiety by shifting from one foot to another, waving your arms around, or conversely being too rigid.
7. **Avoid laughing nervously:** Smile if it's appropriate, but if you giggle or laugh you won't look as if you mean what you say. This will confuse the person you are speaking to.
8. **Don't whine or be sarcastic:** Be direct and honest. Whining and pleading can either annoy the person or make them feel guilty. That is being manipulative. Begin sarcastic, on the other-hand, communicates hostility as you put the other person down.

BASIC ASSERTIVENESS

The following is a basic formula that can be applied to any situation where you feel a need to assert yourself. The formula has five levels of communication and each level serves a vital purpose in communicating across your needs. The following scenario will be used to demonstrate the formula below.

"A work colleague has left the organisation and as a result his/her work responsibilities have been handed over to you to manage in addition to your own position responsibilities. As a result, you have become very stressed as you have had to increase your pace and work longer hours to be able to complete all these responsibilities."

Step 1	You need to identify your need, e.g., reduce your workload back to that outlined in your normal position description.
Step 2	You need to accept that you have the right to meet that need.
Step 3	Work out the script you will use to communication that need across to the person using the formula below.

THE ASSERTIVENESS FORMULA:

Level 1	**Start with a Positive Comment** Purpose: To prevent the other person from becoming defensive. Example: "I really enjoy working here and I love my job but...."
Level 2	**Give a Clear Explanation of the Problem** Purpose: To give a clear explanation of what the problem or issue is. Example: "....ever since Mary left, my workload has increased and ....."
Level 3	**Explain how the Problem is Affecting you on an Emotional Level** Purpose: To ensure the person understands the severity of the problem and why you feel the need to bring it to their attention. Example: ".....I feel very stressed/resentful/ taken for granted etc
Level 4	**Consequence or Loss to the other person if this Problem Continued to Occur** Purpose: To ensure steps aimed at addressing the problem will occur. Making it the other person's problem and responsibility to change the situation. Example: "......If I continue to feel this way (stressed) I will have no other choice but to find another job which I don't really want to do
Level 5	**Negotiation of a Solution Purpose: To achieve a win-win outcome** Example: If the boss explains that he has no one else to do these tasks and promises to fill the position so that you do not have to do any additional tasks on top of your own job responsibilities, but informs you that it will take some time to find a suitable person for the job, it is still his responsibility and not your problem. Therefore, in that situation, you would tell him that he would have to remove some of your tasks and delegate them to other staff members so that you can better manage the additional tasks of the other position. You would also give him a deadline, until which you will be able to assist him with this matter.

ACTIVITY

ACTIVITY 9D:

Apply the Basic Assertiveness Formula described in the previous page to address the Scenarios below:

1. You are watching a movie, but people seated in front of you are making it hard to hear the movie.
2. At a meeting one of your work colleagues often interrupts you when you are speaking.
3. You'd like to ask your boss for a pay rise.
4. You have talked with your boss about a helpful suggestion for organising the work in the office. He says that he thinks it is a good idea and he will ask someone else to put the change into effect but you want to do the job yourself.
5. You are looking forward to a quiet night alone. A relative calls and asks you to baby sit.
6. Your parents or in-laws call and tell you they are dropping by. You are busy.
7. Two workers in your office have been talking about personal matters. The work is piling up. Others have been complaining. You are their supervisor.
8. A good friend is always late for things you plan to do together. You have not said anything for several weeks.
9. A date and time is being set for a weekly meeting. The time is not convenient for you. The times are set when it will be next to impossible for you to make the meeting regularly.
10. Your partner works the same amount of hours you do outside of home but does not contribute to the household chores.

CHAPTER TEN

PERSONALITIES

"Don't change so people will like you. Be yourself and the right people will love the real you"

DEVELOPING a healthy self-esteem can only result in you finding your true self. That is the person you are meant to be and live your life according to. Knowing your true strengths and weakness and your likes and dislikes, will make it easier for you to create a life that 'fits you'. Throughout our life we are faced with a lot of external influences (parents, teachers, peers, partners et cetera), and these influences can contribute to our confusion about what is really best for us. This can often cause internal conflicts between *'what we feel is right'* and *'what we think is right'*. How many times have you done something that just isn't you? Or behaved or dressed in a way that didn't feel comfortable, not exactly you? Or felt that you just didn't click with someone? From a young age we are coached on how to behave, think and feel, and we adapt ourselves accordingly. We do this to 'fit in' and to 'be accepted by others'. In doing so, we end up losing our true self - we continue through life *'drifting in and out of situations'* and *'adapting to whoever and whatever comes into our life at the time'*. Going through life continuously feeling uncomfortable and unhappy because you are a 'round peg' trying to fit into a 'square hole' will inevitably lead to living a life of existence rather than living a life that is right for you.

While we cannot escape our responsibilities, the *'shoulds'* in our life, we can balance our life to also include our *'wants'* – the things that bring us stimulation, fulfillment, enjoyment, purpose, and happiness. If our life is just full of 'shoulds', all responsibility and no fun, then how can we be happy. We are often so conditioned to be overly responsible, that we end up even taking on responsibility that may not even be our own. This only leaves us with no time to slot in the things that we need in life to be happy. We can be so focused on making sure that others are happy, that we forget to focus on our own happiness. Taking on someone else's responsibility when they are capable of doing it themselves, is over-pleasing. Putting yourself out for someone else's convenience, is over-pleasing. Over-pleasing only develops dependency, expectations, laziness, and incompetence in others, and will leave you feeling unvalued when the same is not returned. Balancing our 'wants' and 'shoulds' can be difficult, particularly if self-esteem is low and we find it difficult to say no. Or if we can only feel worthy by achieving and being productive. When you have a healthy self-esteem and you know what you want out of life, getting it is a lot easier. Hence the importance of developing a healthy self-esteem.

A healthy self-worth will enable you to be yourself and to live life in the best way you can. And while having a healthy self-esteem will make it easier to *'get'* what you want out of life, understanding yourself truly will make it easier for you to *'know'* what you want out of life. Understanding your personality is as important as it is having a healthy self-esteem.

We are all born uniquely and yet somehow expected by society to all be the same. There are so many external factors from the time we are born that forge us to be the people we are today. From a young age we are taught what is normal. But what dictates normality? Is it normal to go against our grain and pretend throughout our life to be happy? How many people are living life feeling that they are *'different'* and perhaps feeling *'abnormal'* because they feel different? How can feeling that something is right or wrong be abnormal? Maybe, we should be spending more time listening to what we feel is right for us, instead of only listening to what others 'tell us' is right for us. No one knows us better than we know ourselves. Unfortunately, some of us spend a great part of our life either trying to find ourselves or adapting to it in order to cope with it in the best way we know how. One of the biggest mistakes we can make in life is to change ourselves to fit in life, rather than fitting life to our personality. Our whole life should reflect our personality, our social, work, hobbies and relationships. Life is a lot easier to live when you are doing what comes naturally, and around people who think similarly to you, or when you're differences are accepted by others.

The old saying that 'opposites attract' can in my opinion only work when both parties accept and work with each other's differences instead of trying to change one another. In some relationships when two people are quite different in personalities, the passive person will be more inclined to adapt their personality to the dominant person's. To them, avoiding conflicts might seem a lot less painful than it is to be someone they are not.

Unfortunately, as children we are at the mercy of those that we look up to and rely on for guidance, and while these people may have the best intention for us, they may not always have the best idea nor the right approach. For example, the highly structured parent or teacher may try to encourage the unstructured child to think and behave in a way that they believe is best for the child, not realising the struggle that that child might be having trying to be someone that they might not be able to be. As such, we grow up knowing that as adults we should be able to live the life we want, but find ourselves unable to do so due to an invisible barrier – *the conditioning* we had that keeps us doing what we know will be approved by others rather than what will make us happy. Only once you let go of the need to please, will you then start to live the life you want to live.

PERSONALITY DIFFERENCES

I first become very interested in personality differences when I noticed a correlation between personality identity crisis' and mental illness. Over the last twenty years as a private practicing psychologist, I found myself explaining to many parents that there was nothing wrong with their child, and that what they thought was learning difficulties or defiant behaviour or even symptoms of Asperger Syndrome was in fact, that they were highly creative children.

We are all creative in some way, however some of us are more creative and therefore, display 'highly creative personality traits' that are often misunderstood as 'weaknesses' or worse still, symptoms. Highly creative people (HCP) can differ to Average Creative People (ACP) in the way they think, behave, learn, socialise, relate to others, and live their life. ACPs are a lot more structured then HCPs, and this can become a problem for HCPs particularly during their childhood when they are forced to behaviour and think more like an ACP by parents and teachers. The teaching system is highly structured and tend to teach using a more auditory than visual approach. Auditory learning is a learning style in which a person learns through listening. An auditory learner depends on hearing and speaking as a main way of learning. On the contrary, visual learning is a learning style in which ideas, concepts, data, and other information is associated with images and techniques. A student who is a visual learner will often find learning the auditory way very difficult, and can fall behind as a result. Most HCPs cope with primary school years until Grade 3 when the teaching style becomes less visual and more auditory. A visual learner may find it very difficult to concentrate and process too many words or follow instructions that are too wordy, and this is often misinterpreted as a concentration or learning problem. I often prove this to parents by asking the child to recall a list of ten items that I give them. When I ask them to recall the list immediately after reading it, they fail at the task significantly. However, when I instruct them to visualise each item I read out to them, and ask them to recall the list at the end of the one-hour session, they are able to recall all ten items. This is because a visual learner needs to encode words into their short-term memory in a visual manner. A HCP will display the following common behaviours that will drive a teacher up the wall; they will rush writing their story and forget punctuation, or proper letter formation, because they believe that their "creative" story is the most important part of the exercise, they will be often caught out daydreaming, put only efforts into the assignments that interest them only, their projects will have more visuals (eg., diagrams and pictures) then words (eg., storyline), they are untidy and disorganised, and fidget and tap and doodle. All of this can be easily misunderstood as symptoms that can land them in therapy or unfortunately cause them to fall through the net. HCP are highly intelligent and very capable people who are often let down by the education system that does not cater for their learning style. Further research is much needed to explore how incorporating a visual teaching style within the education system might help highly creative people to learn more effectively and develop into healthy minded people.

COMMON TRAITS OF A HIGHLY CREATIVE PERSON

While there are many books on personality differences including the well-known Myers Briggs, that explain how and why we think and behave, I prefer to concentrate on the differences between the Highly Creative Personality and the Average Creative Personality. It is much easier and straight forward to compare apples to oranges, instead of comparing apples to many different fruit.

Highly Creative People I found to be typically;

Disorganised. They tend to be more organised for the things they consider to be most important to them or more critical.

Untidy: They tend to be very untidy and find it more comfortable to live in a 'mess' or 'dishevel' and to others' surprise able to always know where to find what they are looking for. Because they don't have their minds occupied with a 'to do list' they are able to pay attention more on their actions.

Introvert: They tend to keep more to themselves and prefer their own company than that of others. They find it difficult to talk 'small talk' and prefer to engage in deep meaningful and interesting conversations instead. They spend a lot of time in their own company and may have one or two close relationships.

Bored easily: They tend to require and seek constant stimulation. As kids they will ask a lot of questions especially curly ones. Like "what makes the blue colour in the sky? or the yellow colour in the flames of a fire?". They enjoy researching on any topic in depth. Unfortunately, they can rely on food to pick up any negative mood including boredom. Parents can become very frustrated at their child's strong interest in playing computer games. Even as adults, HCP will seek strategic gaming as a means of maintaining stimulation particularly, in times of boredom.

Live in the now: They tend to find it difficult to plan ahead or to set goals for their future and often seen as immature or lazy for this reason. They are happy to live a simplistic and practical life and not materialistic.

Practical: They tend to live and dress practically and their lack of interest in fashion and material things are not always understood by others. They dress for comfort and practicality not appearance. Females are often viewed as 'tomboys' for this reason.

Visual: They tend to appreciate beauty and colour and tangible things, the things that others often take for granted like landscape. They are more likely to remember the food they ate and what they saw while travelling then what they did.

Unable to commit: They tend to find it difficult to commit to something for fear of changing their minds or not being in the mood when the time comes. You'll hear them saying, "I'll see how I feel" when you are trying to organise a social activity with them.

Not career focused: They tend to find working to be a tool to living the life they need and as such, tend to not be career minded. For some, their ideal life would be to work part-time only or not at all if that was possible, and fill most of their time with their hobbies and recreational activities.

Unmotivated: They tend to only be motivated by passion or consequence. Parents of highly creative kids find it difficult to motivate them to do things they're not interested in like homework. This is often misinterpreted as laziness. Highly creative kids are more likely to respond to consequence than reward or praise for example, having privileges taken away. Parents will find this form of discipline at times unsuccessful because creative children have the ability to use their imagination to entertain themselves, and are often not affected by the consequence. I will often have parents say "I can take away everything and it won't even affect them".

Easily distracted: They tend to be easily distracted. Parents of highly creative children will find it frustrating to get them ready for school in the morning because they might intend to do what they are asked to but along the way become distracted by things that grab their interest.

Logical: They tend to think before they act and will weigh things up before engaging in anything. They are quite mature as children and seek out the company of adults or older children. Unfortunately, they're maturity sometimes is camouflaged by the other characteristics mentioned above.

Down to earth: They tend to be very genuine and down to earth people who find it difficult to put their trust in others that they do not find do the same.

Manipulate: They tend to be very good at manipulating others to get what they want. Their overall personality tends to make them appear helpless, and this can result in the development of dependency on others, often instigated by others not them.

Difficulties inhibiting urges: What they do, tends to be strongly influenced by their moods, therefore, they can find it difficult to control their urges particularly when it comes to food or spending.

CHAPTER ELEVEN

START LIVING

"Remember: Whatever you believe about yourself on the inside, is what you will manifest on the outside".

LIVING with Depression and/Anxiety is debilitating. The common feeling described by suffers are that of feeling 'trapped', 'lost', 'hopelessness', 'helplessness', and of being a 'burden' on their loved ones'. Even with the right intention of helping and supporting, without fully understanding the condition and by taking the wrong approach, loved ones can without realising, aggravate these negative feelings. The most important thing to remember is that Depression and Anxiety are not conditions brought on by the suffer, nor are they easy to control and treat. This self-help book does not claim to 'cure' Depression or Anxiety, it was written to help people manage their symptoms better, and to provide them with the skills to cope with these conditions more effectively. This book can be useful when used in conjunction with therapy. It was written with the goal of providing more insight about these conditions and an explanation about some of the contributing factors, coping strategies to manage, particularly in promoting healthier thinking patterns. Correcting thinking to a more objective and healthier approach can be effective in drawing the correct conclusions made on evidence collected rather than on assumptions. We can grow our negativity like a virus simply by relying on what we think and feel is going on, instead of what is actually going on.

Our emotions and physical responses are controlled by our thinking, this is why it is vital that our thinking and interpretation of all incoming information are accurate and not based solely on our subjective interpretations. By remembering to assess everything that you think, feel, all external comments you receive, and all outcomes both positively and negatively, in an objective manner, you will ensure that the interpretations that you make will be real, and you can respond in the way you need to respond.

Remember, you are what you think. Your mind controls the chemicals your brain releases, and your brain controls how your body responds. If you think negatively you will feel and respond in a negative way, if you think positively, you will feel and respond accordingly. Thinking positively is not a simple matter of just thinking it or rehearsing positive affirmations, it involves actually believing that what you are thinking is actually true, and to determine if it is true, you need to have the evidence that supports it – *evidence that is, outside of what you think and feel.* Simply, just saying to yourself that you are attractive but not having the evidence to support that thought is not going to work. Looking for evidence outside of yourself such as, the compliments, criticisms and/or lack of criticisms about your appearance is a more accurate means of drawing that opinion of yourself, rather than relying solely on what you think others may think or on just one or two people's criticism. Drawing conclusions on the majority rather than the minority is a much more accurate way.

Correcting unhealthy thinking requires practice and the homework provided throughout this book will provide this. Doing the homework and activities on a daily basis will help to develop that healthier thinking pattern. Overtime

time, you should find it easier to do and notice less negative thinking and with that more positive feelings. The more positive you feel the more you will want to step out of your comfort zone and start to live and grow.

APPENDICES

APPENDIX A

TRUE Evidence for: *Evidence supporting the criticism*	FALSE Evidence against: *Evidence supporting that the criticism is false*
•	•
•	•
•	•
•	•
•	•
•	•
•	•
•	•
•	•
•	•
•	•
•	•
•	•
•	•
•	•
•	•

APPENDIX B

HOMEWORK 8A:

Apply the 'What if" formula to situations in the past that you may have responded to in an over-reactive manner.

***Exercise 1:** What If Exercise*

What if (situation):

____

____

____

____

____

What is the likelihood of that this situation will occur? (collect objective information, do not rely on what you think or feel).

____

____

____

____

____

[Low] / [Medium] / [High]

How much of an impact will it have on you should it occur? (collect objective information, do not rely on what you think or feel).

____

____

____

____

____

[Low] / [Medium] / [High]

REFERENCES

BOOKS

Jeffery, Douglas R., M.D., Ph.D. "Nutrition and Diseases of the Nervous System." In *Modern Nutrition in Health and Disease.* 9th edition. Edited by Maurice E. Shils, M.D., Sc.D., James A. Olson, Ph.D., Moshe Shike, M.D., and A. Catharine Ross, Ph.D. Baltimore: Williams and Wilkins, 1999.

Katz, David L., M.D., M.P.H. *Nutrition in Clinical Practice.* New York: Lippincott, Williams, and Wilkins, 2001.

Shiveley, LeeAnn R., M.P.H, R.D. and Patrick J. Connolly, M.D. "Medical Nutrition Therapy for Neurologic Disorders." In *Krause's Food, Nutrition, & Diet Therapy.* 10th edition. Edited by L. Kathleen Mahan, M.S., R.D.,C.D.E., and Sylvia Escott-Stump, M.A., R.D., L.D.N. New York: W. B. Saunders Company, 2000.

Westermarck T., M.D., D.Sc. and E. Antila, M.D., Ph.D. "Diet in Relation to the Nervous System." In *Human Nutrition and Dietetics.* 10th edition. Edited by J. S. Garrow, M.D., Ph.D., W. P. T. James, M.D., S.Sc., and A. Ralph, Ph.D. New York: Churchill Livingstone, 2000.

PERIODICALS

Young, Simon N. "Clinical Nutrition: 3. The Fuzzy Boundary Between Nutrition and Psychopharmacology." *Canadian Medical Association Journal* 166 (2002): 205-209.

ORGANISATIONS

American Dietetic Association. 216 West Jackson Boulevard, Chicago, Illinois, 60606-6995.

http://www.eatright.org

Nancy Gustafson, M.S., R.D., F.A.D.A., E.L.S. Read more:

http://www.minddisorders.com/Kau-Nu/Nutrition- and-mental- health.html#ixzz0SXTXcZNc

WEBSITES (SOURCES)

http://www.minddisorders.com/Kau-Nu/Nutrition- and-mental- health.html

http://mental.healthguru.com/video/how-do- antidepressants-work

http://commonantidepressants.weebly.com/selective-serotonin- reuptake-inhibitors.html

Printed in Great Britain
by Amazon